Parenting Forever

Linda Roehrig Knapp

Copyright © 2017 Linda Roehrig Knapp

All rights reserved. No part of this publication may be reproduced or transmitted in any form or by any means, electronic or mechanical, including photocopy, recording, or information storage and retrieval systems without permission in writing from the publisher.

ISBN # 978-0-9979695-1-1

Published by Beverly Creek Press
10925 Kulshan Road
Woodway, WA 98020

Acknowledgements: Thank you, Mike, for your cartoons depicting special times in our family.
And thank you, Justin, for the front cover photo.
Also thanks to the websites that offer free images.

Printed by Amazon,
CreateSpace, a DBA of On-Demand Publishing, LLC

The typefaces used in this book are Bernhard Modern BT and Avenir Next.

Parenting Forever

Linda Roehrig Knapp

Beverly Creek Press
Woodway, Washington

Dedication

To Michael, my partner in parenting—the adventure that once it begins, never ends . . .
Thank you for encouraging me to take on this project and serving as its editor and producer.

Also to Justin, Molly, and Abby, for enduring our parenting, and still managing to grow up to be terrific adults.

Books by Linda Roehrig Knapp

Non-Fiction:

- *The Word Processor and the Writing Teacher*, by Linda Roehrig Knapp, Prentice-Hall, Inc., 1986.
- *Restructuring Schools with Technology*, by Linda Roehrig Knapp & Allen D. Glenn, Allyn& Bacon, 1996.

Fiction:

- *Search*, by Linda Knapp, BookSurge, 2007.
- *Their Secrets*, by Linda Knapp, BookSurge, 2008.

Autobiographical:

- *Hearing Without Ears*, by Linda Knapp, BookSurge, 2009.
- *Parenting Forever*, by Linda Roehrig Knapp, Beverly Creek Press, 2017.

Contents

Preface: Just to Let You Know — 1

Part One: The Full House (1992—1998) — 5

1. Monday Morning — 7
2. Sports for Personal Growth and High Fashion — 11
3. *Liberated* has a New Meaning — 17
4. Middle-aged . . . Me? — 21
5. Creative Child Confounds Mom with Graffiti — 25
6. Who's Obsessed with Technology? — 29
7. You're Really Ready to Go Steady? — 33
8. Hurray—It's Homework Time — 39
9. First Born, Last Born, Does it Really Matter? — 45
10. Scamper to the Bookshelf — 51
11. Danger Zone: Party in Progress — 55
12. Some Gifts are more Precious than Presents — 59
13. Hairy Home Styles — 63
14. TV: Should Mom Turn it Off? — 67
15. Bedroom Disaster — 71
16. Skinheads in My Living Room — 75
17. Readers Respond to 'Skinheads' Column — 79
18. Teen Hotel Party Tests Parental Trust — 83
19. Adopting Kids is a Great Way to Create a Family — 87
20. One Plus One = Trouble — 91
21. Pregnant at 48? Yikes! — 95
22. Smoking Once, Smoking Twice — 99
23. Classroom Mothers Are My Heroes — 103

24 Required Volunteer Service	107
25 The Daycare Divide	111
26 A Storm in December	115
27 Liberated Couple	119
28 I Love the Internet!	123
29 Kindergarten Literary Practice	127
30 How Blind is Color Blind?	131
Part Two: The Emptying Nest (1999—2002)	135
31 What Happens When Mom Tries to Cook?	137
32 Clever Child Earns an Economic Edge	141
33 How Can We Stop Youth Violence?	145
34 Mother-Daughter Dreams, Realities	149
35 If it's Free, Just Say No	153
36 Beginning Computing = Advanced Frustration	157
37 Sweating My Way	161
38 Why Do We Have Pets?	165
39 Monsters in Our Midst	169
40 Until Divorce Do Us Part	173
41 Millennium Woman at Age Six	177
42 Kids on Computers: When is it Too Soon?	181
43 Thinking on the Surface, and Thinking Deep	185
44 We Pulled the Plug	189
45 Generation Gaps and Bridges	193
46 True Confessions of Computer Love & Logic	197
47 A Little Lapse of Manners	201
48 A Mother's New Groove	205
49 The Great Pokémon Turn-Off	209
50 Too Much Emphasis on Testing?	213
51 Back on a Mac	217

52 What to Do with a Reluctant Swimmer	221
53 Waiting to Fly, Again	225
54 How Important are Pets?	229
55 Getting Connected with a Wireless Phone	233
56 Thoughts on Living with Terrorism	237
57 Finding that Holiday Feeling Again	241
58 Learning to Type	245
59 The Ritalin Dilemma	249
60 Heroes, Role Models, Mentors	253
61 The Modern Little Red Schoolhouse	257
62 Home Course in Film History	261
63 Anxiety at Home is a Growing Concern	265
64 A Tale of Two Photo	269
65 Escape from Technology	271
Afterword: Two Decades Later	275

Preface:
Just to Let You Know . . .

This book is for parents—past, present, and future. It's mainly a collection of columns (1997-2002) that I wrote for *The Enterprise*, a Seattle-area newspaper, about parenting three kids ranging in age from 3 to 16 when the columns begin, with further parental commentary and perspective added two decades later.

These columns present parenting issues common to many parents of kids growing up then and now, from what to do with a toddler who draws on her bedroom walls; to how to encourage a teenager to talk with you about what's really happening with his friends, and then helping him decide to make good choices even when his friends make not-so-good ones. Or, how to encourage and enable your high school kid to spend enough time on homework even when exhausted from school and sports. And sometimes, just to support your daughter as she learns to navigate the dating world and enter

Parenting Forever

relationships with partners she can have fun with, respect, and trust.

Each column is a brief episode, or story about our family from 1993 (when our last child was born) through 2002 (with a flashback to our first child's arrival in 1980).

Now, in 2016, I've added comments at the end of many columns about how our lives, and the kids', have changed over time. We're a pretty normal middle-class family, without celebrity status, notoriety, or extreme circumstances to put us on the evening news. Perhaps we're a lot like you.

The main characters are my three kids. When the stories begin they are 3, 15, and 16 years-old. That's a wide age range, so the columns include issues that parents face when we have young children, and when the kids are teenagers, and in their early 20s.

As the columns (and the years) progress, our older two go off to college, our nest becomes emptier, and I begin focusing on issues beyond parenting. But, of course, some parenting issues continue even when the kids spend less time at home . . . This book's title is *Parenting Forever*, because as my husband and I have discovered over the past 36 years, once you become a parent, you're always a parent.

Now for a little background information . . .

Mike and I met in Malawi, Africa, where we were both Peace Corps Volunteers, met again in Boston where we were both graduate students, met lots more times for fun, and married in 1976. Then we drove to California where Mike began a doctoral program in Education, and I a teaching job at a local college.

Preface

    Not so many years later, after failed efforts to conceive a baby, we adopted an infant boy, and a year later an infant girl. I quit my teaching job to be at home with the kids . . .

    But not so very long after that, I decided to go back to work. I loved being a mom, but not a totally fulltime mom. I got a job teaching English part-time at a local college, and wrote articles for personal computing magazines and then complete issues of *Apple Education News*. A couple years later, I joined Apple fulltime as a Senior Writer/Communications Manager for their education research project, Apple Classrooms of Tomorrow (ACOT).

    After a few years of high-pressure work with much travel to our experimental schools around the country, and Mike's frequent travel for his educational research firm, he decided to try teaching, and got a job as associate professor of education at the University of Washington. My colleagues told me that NOBODY leaves a job at Apple and so, of course, I should become a commuter, spending my weekdays at Apple and my weekends at home in WA. No. Definitely not for me. I left Apple with my husband's offer that I could be free to work or not, and he would support us.

    We moved to Shoreline, just north of Seattle, where the schools were reportedly good and the commute to UW quite doable. In the fall, Justin entered 5th grade and Molly 4th grade. Surprise, surprise, a couple of years later I got pregnant, and Abby was born. Three years after that, I started writing the "Family Affairs," later re-titled "Over Coffee," column for *The Enterprise* newspaper, and a few years later began writing the "Getting Started" column about personal technology for *The Seattle Times*.

✻

Parenting Forever

Now, in 2016, the kids have agreed to let me use their real names rather than the pseudo ones I originally used in the columns, but they requested that I tell you that the columns do not represent their points-of-view and aren't always 100% accurate. I'll also add that now, as parents themselves (two of them anyway), their own parenting is excellent.

Part One:
The Full House
(1992—1998)

Monday Morning

It's 6:15 Monday morning. No one else is up yet. This is my time to exercise and catch up on the news before alarms go off and bodies begin to fill the kitchen. So, I'm working out on my exercise machine while watching CNN when Molly's voice surprises me from the hallway: "Can I borrow your shower cap?"

Just give me two more minutes, I'm thinking. But, of course, I have to answer. "Why can't you use your own? I just bought you one."

"I can't find it."

"Last time you borrowed mine, I found it two weeks later under your bed." I glance at the clock, get off the machine, turn off the TV, and head for the kitchen.

Molly follows. She opens a drawer and pulls out a roll of plastic wrap. "I'll use this," she mutters, measuring a section to cover her head.

"Geeze. Okay, forget it," I mutter back. "You can use mine, but please return it this time."

Now that I'm feeling sufficiently guilty for being ungenerous, Molly can borrow with a clear conscience. This 15-year-old is famous for using my things and then losing them. Thank goodness she's bigger than I am now and there isn't much she can borrow.

So why do I feel guilty? She's the one who doesn't return what she borrows. Still, I want to start the day off better, so I reach out and start tickling. That never fails. She wriggles away and heads for the shower.

It takes 15 minutes to unload the dishwasher, make two ham and cheese sandwiches and bag them along with pretzels, granola bars, apples, muffins and juice. Five more minutes to fill my cereal bowl and Abby's, start the coffee, cut fruit slices, and pour milk. At 6:50 I let the dogs out and go upstairs to fetch the 3 year-old.

Ten minutes later my youngest and I are munching cereal at the table, Molly is making toast and Justin is discovering—once again—that when he adds milk to a heaping bowl of cereal, it floods. He's 16.

I hand him a sponge.

"All set for playschool?" Molly asks, approaching her little sister with a hairbrush.

"Oh yes!"

"Want me to put your hair in pony tails?"

"Oh no!"

"But what if I put blue bows on your ponies?"

"Okay." So Molly starts brushing. But it's snarly this morning, and Abby is impatient.

"No, don't," she protests, shaking her head.

Monday Morning

It's nearly impossible to lasso bucking ponies, so Molly has to surrender to the wisdom of maybe tomorrow. She puts the bows on Abby's doggie slippers and heads for the bathroom to fix her own hair.

I'm thankful for the 12 years between them which helps keep peace around here. It took Molly and Justin at least that many years to have practically any interaction without tears.

My husband, Mike, moves amiably to and from the breakfast table and deposits his dishes in the dishwasher. Good enough. Once they showed up in the fridge; another time I found them in the dishwasher, right-side up with some cereal and milk still in the bowl.

Justin has finished eating, so it's safe to approach him now. "Dad won't be able to pick you up until 5:00. Will you please study at school after vocal practice? You have three tests tomorrow."

I know there's zero chance he'll study, but I keep hoping.

He smiles. Good sign. But then he slides into his comedy routine, adding fancy steps and making up a rhyme about it not being cool to study at school.

"Just study, okay?" I push him toward the door. It takes an effort to look stern.

He detours to the bathroom to check out zits (none evident) and smile in the mirror. "Aren't you lucky I'm so handsome."

"Goodbye, Justin!" Mike and Molly are already waiting in the car. It's at least a 30-minute drive to their school in downtown Seattle.

An hour later, Abby and I arrive at her preschool. We say hello to some kids, and Abby heads for the reading corner where we read *Three Little Pigs*, while she collects her own mental bricks to build a safe house at school. When it's time for me to leave, there's a quick hug and a kiss. Then, her muscles stiffen and she looks the other way. My cue to exit. Soon it will be easier to say goodbye; I know she has a good time here.

Back home, I brew a second cup of coffee and smile. The next few hours are all mine.

Papers scattered on my desk and a glowing computer screen welcome me to work. I sit down and sip warm espresso. The phone rings and I don't answer it.

Now, 20 years later, Justin has two sons of his own who may not flood their cereal bowls with too much milk, but we've seen the older son dance with his dad's skill and grace many evenings after dinner. Molly has a son, and a daughter who proudly wears bows in her hair and on her slippers. Abby is so far unmarried, forging her own way as an expert karate competitor and sensei.

Sports for Personal Growth
and High Fashion

My son Justin has been playing soccer and baseball for 12 years, basketball for 8, and other sports between seasons. Those numbers are impressive when employers look for job experience on a resume. But he's a high school kid, and we're talking sports here, not employment. For Justin, sports is his work. His school. His present and his future. Whatever profession he chooses, it will probably have something to do with sports.

In the early years, Justin's natural ability made it too easy for him to be one of the top players. This promoted a kind of cocky confidence, but not a consistent work ethic. He put out for games, but goofed off at practice. Then, some of those players who sat on the bench in sixth grade, began to beat his batting average because they practiced harder. So, Justin went to work. Now he sweats for his starting positions, and generally keeps them, thanks to excellent coaching and an engine that revs for the starting lineup.

How do parents fit into this picture? We're the fuzzy little figures in the background; the ones holding his jacket and the bag of orange rinds. But we're there, and we support his involvement 100 percent. Not because we have any ambition for him to be a star athlete, we don't, but because we affirm his ambition to excel at something he loves. And because we believe that sports—when coached by adults who care more about improving players than scores—have helped Justin become a better person.

My husband has been a referee, scorekeeper and chauffeur, season after prolonged season. My role has always been carpool driver to afternoon practice and supportive spectator. The sports arena is an ideal place to network with other parents, and cheer for my child as well. In the process, I've developed a talent for catching up on gossip, while still managing to see Justin steal the ball and sink a basket.

Parent gossip, by the way, is essential stuff. It's our ticket to maintaining respect and control of the kids. If I know what's going on around school, it's much harder for Justin to pull a fast one. "But NOBODY else has to be home by 12:00," doesn't fly when I have the facts. And if I know which schoolmates are drinking, I know enough to check on Justin when he's out with them. To get this vital information, I may miss some artful plays, but I don't miss the important moments. I know exactly when to glance over at the game to see my son make a brilliant move.

At the last basketball game, I was chatting with another mom about the drinking scene. We know which two kids are the primary boozers, and their mothers don't believe they

Sports for Growth and High Fashion

drink. The issue for us is whether to tell those moms the truth. We'd want to know if our kids were drinking. In a flash, my eyes are under our basket as Justin steals the ball and leaps for a shot. Yes! The conversation has ended between to tell or not to tell. It's tricky when the evidence comes from a kid. If I tell, it's Justin who ends up with the rap, for telling me. I'm cautious about what I say; I want my kids to keep talking.

Whenever Justin begins a season with a new uniform, I wonder what inspires the designers of athletic clothing. Think about it. Have you ever seen a team uniform your kids would wear anywhere besides a game? Soccer shirts are like neon signs, and the shorts hang to long skinny socks with stripes.

Basketball uniforms repeat the saggy soccer disaster, with a change of footwear. Shoes on the court look like little racing cars—brassy stripes, aerodynamic curves, and a forward tilt. They're only missing headlights and a rear-view mirror.

When baseball arrives, there's a fashion shift, from baggy to clingy around the thighs. Add useless garters, canoe-like cleats, and shirt modeled after a pillowcase, and you have the athlete's wardrobe for all seasons—baggy boxers to little leggings. Now, if these fashions are designed to attract attention, they do. Like peacock feathers and Halloween costumes.

–I have to cut in here, as it wasn't too many years after this column that athletes' shirts and shorts and shoes became fashionable for kids to wear off the field/court/diamond, even by those who don't play sports–

So why are sports so special—better than music, art, or any other involvement that helps kids develop talent, a work ethic, and self-esteem? They're not. They're simply the right match for my son.

Through sports, he's learning to follow instructions, collaborate with peers, build skills, become a leader, value good health—the whole spiel we get from advice books and athletic departments. But what they say is absolutely true for Justin. He's a living advertisement for sports programs. He could be a troublemaker now if he wasn't an athlete. This kid needs a place to put his energy, to learn how to manage powerful emotions, and to win and lose with dignity.

School hasn't been as successful in fulfilling Justin's needs as participating in sports. That's why we spend Friday nights in the gym and endless weekends beside the field. We're promoting his education, almost as much as if we were sitting in back of the classroom and cheering while he solves a trigonometry problem.

Indeed, I wonder why there's no cheering section at school and little encouragement to attend the academic games they play there. I can picture myself sitting at the back of a classroom, quietly attentive as my child aces a history quiz. And to top it off, there's no history uniform.

Later in high school, Justin's passion evolved from performing on the field, to performing on stage, and by the time he was a senior he'd earned the starring role in the school play, "Guys and Dolls." In college, he started as a

Sports for Growth and High Fashion

Communications major and later switched to Drama where he acted, directed, designed stage lighting, and a lot more.

He's still devoted to sports—watching many professional teams play, and coaching his son's baseball team. Plus, he plays darts, and his team often does well in tournaments.

I'm happy to add that there's no darts team uniform.

> **Emergency Information**
>
> Father's Name: Mike Knapp   Home Phone: 206-544-5616
> Work Address: 1126 Bancroft St   Work Phone: 206-409-9732
> Profession: Professor
>
> Mother's Name: Linda Knapp   Home Phone: 206-544-5666
> Home Address: 1234 Webster St   Work Phone: — Home —
> Work Address: — Home —
> Profession: Housewife
>
> Doctor: D Childs   Phone: 206-449-3366
> Dentist: Dr Bennett   Phone: 206-602-2345
>
> Adults on the trip have permission to apply emergency treatment to
> Molly if it becomes necessary while on the trip.
>
> Parent Signature: _____

Liberated has a New Meaning

Just back from school, Molly saunters into the kitchen wearing cut-off jeans, silver nail polish, and hiking boots.

"Hey, Molly, how was the Alaska trip meeting?"

"Fine, Mom. Got something for you."

Backpack to the floor, she pulls out a piece of paper and hands it over. "You need to sign this."

It's a parent permission slip requesting emergency information, like so many I've signed, with spaces for father's and mother's work titles, addresses, and phone numbers. But this time I notice Molly's written Housewife beside my name.

My head shoots up as I look at her. "Why didn't you put Writer? I react. "I've published two books and 100 articles. What do you think I do all day while you're away?" I'm squeaking like a trapped mouse, lashing out and disclaiming what I really am to the kids, just plain Mom.

"Sor-rey," she says, and the grin grows—my clue that she did it on purpose to get a rise out of me. A baited trap and I jumped right in. Molly goes off chuckling, while I madly chop vegetables.

I grew up in the early '60s when girls had to wear skirts to school, and boys wore pressed pants. Girls waited for boys to call them on the phone, and boys paid for their movies. I came home to a mother who was always there for me. She'd be sitting in that old easy chair with a cup of coffee, a book in her lap, and Beethoven in the background. I'd race in to tell her about the surprise math quiz, or my argument with Tim. She was a trusted confidante, and encouraged me to do more with my life than she had done with hers. But I thought she was perfect.

Today, that role model is out of style. Yet, in all my attempts to mold myself into a more fashionable example for my own children, I cannot. I have tried. When my kids were small I worked freelance, and then took on a bigger job at Apple Computer.

Terrific, I thought, now I'm a first-class Super Mom. I worked early, late, and on Saturdays. The kids got extra treats and computer games from the office. They even got to ride in a limousine: but they didn't get time to relax at home.

"Quality time" was a popular sound bite in those days, and working mothers thought they didn't need to spend afternoons with their kids as long as they had special time together. So, half an hour of quality time is written into the working mom's schedule. But what happens, of course, is that half hour is not when my child chooses to connect. It takes hours, not minutes, for a kid to feel comfortable enough to let go of feelings. Ultimately, I left the job and retreated again

Liberated has a New Meaning

to freelance writing, so my over-daycared kids could hang out at home.

I'm thankful we can manage half the income, yet I wonder what kind of role model this presents for my '90s children. I want them to understand what it means to be a caring parent and a competent professional, and how to handle both successfully. And I want them to manage better than I have.

Today, women and men have the right to choose—whether we want to have kids, go to work, fix the car, or whatever, as long as we share responsibilities amicably with those we live with. In our family, my husband's primary job is family finance and mine is raising kids. He'd rather balance the checkbook than wash the floor. I'd rather take kids to the dentist than take the cars for oil changes.

If we'd grown up in the liberated '70s, maybe I'd fix the plumbing and he'd stay home when the kids are sick. The point is, back when we grew up, we couldn't choose, and now we can. That makes all the difference.

I'm still cooking dinner when Molly comes waltzing back into the kitchen.

"What do you want to be when you grow up?" This time I set the trap.

"A psychologist," she answers without pause. "And a mom."

Hurrah, I'm thinking as I sign the permission slip. Forget the trap.

She grabs a pencil, writes something on the form, and then shows me the new title beside my name: Mother and Writer.

"Happy, Mom?" she grins.

Parenting Forever

I have a hunch she'll be more comfortable with her own double title, if she becomes a psychologist and a mother.

Twenty years later Molly is quite comfortable with her own double title, Mother & Teacher, and is excellent at both.

Middle-aged . . . Me?

I just turned f-f-fifty. Damn, I can't even write it without cringing. My plan was to write about how fine it feels to be middle-aged, like that prominent MacArthur study reported a few months ago . . . that we're supposed to be thrilled to be this old. The study said that most mid-lifers are content with their marriages, children, and jobs. Well, that may be true, and so is the part about us (40-50 year-olds) being satisfied, even if we haven't accomplished everything we intended to.

It's the part that says we feel many years younger than we look that gets me, as if how we look doesn't matter anymore. It's supposed to be okay to add wrinkles, pounds, and aches at our age. Well, I hate it. The saggy skin and stiff necks. Noticing that I'm casually overlooked in a crowd of younger men and women. Knowing my professional options are diminished. Awkkkkk!

Still, I've no wish to be twenty, or even thirty-something again. Back when it was so critical to push ahead—get a better job, equal pay, promotions, a bigger office. Even at home, judging myself by how well my kids did at school and on the soccer field.

According to Gail Sheehy in *New Passages*, it's pretty common for 20-30 year-olds to be anxious and ambitious, while competing for external approval and success.

Sheehy says when we reach our late 40s or early 50s, we take a horrified look at our aging bodies, professional ceilings, fleeing children, and realize that things are different. (She obviously hadn't read the MacArthur study.) It's identity crisis time, just like when we were teenagers, only now the game's half-played, and so is our future.

The transition is all about finding a new version of attractiveness as well as new personal and professional goals. When we can accept and enjoy our rounder, more mellow selves, we can build on our unique qualities and complexities.

Well, I'm almost there, sort of. I don't care about the big office or the promotions anymore. My ideal work day occurs when I can dress up in blue jeans and meet with my keyboard for eight uninterrupted hours. And now, when my kids come home with low grades, it's their problem we address, not mine. Yes, I definitely feel more relaxed. Plus, I know more, and have more worldly experience than ever before, at fif-f-f . . .

It's the deteriorating body parts that's so hard for me. I want to restore my chassis, like my car—a new engine and a

Middle-aged... Me?

paint job, please. I want to like what I see in the mirror. I want to be noticed at a party. And I want my kids to quit making comments like, "Could surf on those wrinkles, Mom," or "Can't you even touch your toes?" Worse is the innocent, "Why can't you look like Lisa?" The neighbor nearly my age who could be a cover girl for *Fitness* magazine.

Sheehy says some people deal with middle age by giving up. Abandoning earlier controls on eating and drinking, quitting exercise, and ultimately adopting an I-don't-care approach to how they look. Some become chronically depressed.

Forget that. Heck, there's half a life left to go. My body may be heading downhill, but my mind isn't. I've never felt more creative, productive, even wise. According to Sheehy, at our age, we're also more accepting, confident, and outspoken. Yes, Ma'am, loud and clear.

It must be time to laugh at ourselves. Relax and enjoy family, friends, and work.

Maybe it's finally time to grow up and get beyond looks . . . So folks (all of us beyond half time) let's age with attitude. All together now: gray is beautiful, a little flab is fine, wrinkles show wisdom. Then walk, not run, to the mirror. Take a long look, beyond that skin. Now sing out your age . . .

Okay. I'm fif-f . . .

Oh, dear.

Well, I'm 72 now, and just as uncomfortable with my age, but at least I can say it without stuttering. Or, maybe I'm just too old to stutter.

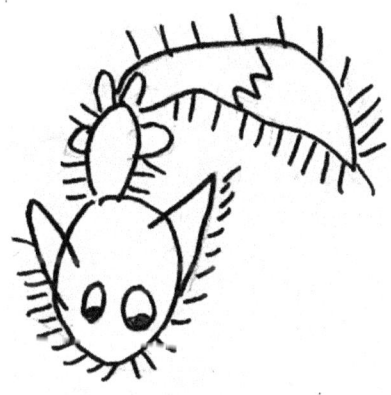

Creative Child Confounds Mom with Graffiti

When I open the door to Abby's room at the end of rest time, I face a wild mass of pink and purple stick people, dogs, and assorted monsters that resembles a museum's cave drawing, but is the furtive work of my expressive, just turned 4 year-old.

The evidence of her adventures over three walls is fantastic. Silently I prize Abby's imagination, while scolding her, removing the chalk, and scrubbing the walls. Once again, my preschool artist has traded the boundaries of her blackboard for the vast canvas of white walls.

Last week I discovered purple trees on her bookcase. I chided her for that, and yesterday found two dancing bunnies inside her closet door. I must admit I've had little success at redirecting her passion for drawing on walls to drawing only on acceptable surfaces. Abby loves to draw on everything.

I expect her logic works like this: if I can write on a wall blackboard, why not the wall? Mom gives me pieces of wood to paint, so my bureau must be fine too. The logic is clear, even rational, I concede. Maybe she really doesn't understand the difference.

But there are clues. She doesn't ask before venturing to draw on forbidden surfaces, and she typically does it during rest time when she's alone with the door closed. I think Abby knows exactly what mischief she's making. I think she is checking the fences, curious to discover what will happen when she jumps over.

A psychologist friends of mine agrees, and suggests it's consequence time.

"Patience," my mother soothes me. "She's only four. You drew daisies all over your brother's crib."

Neither of my other two kids did this kind of underground artistry, and I'm not sure how to stop it, while still promoting Abby's interest in drawing. So far, my solution has been to continue coaching her about what's okay and what isn't, offering plenty of paper, and making sure all available writing materials are washable.

But I see now that she needs a bit more law enforcement than that, and I'll probably banish chalk and markers during rest time until the delinquent artist learns the difference between graffiti and art. Delinquent artist—what a contradiction: she's a vandal and a creator. No wonder I can't decide whether to bug her or hug her for her gifts.

Meanwhile, she'll continue creating, but with close supervision. It's fun to sit with her while she draws, and tells stories while she works. This afternoon she drew a mother with a circle face and stick limbs. Then she drew an egg-shaped duck sitting beside her. The story went like this: "One day Mom said to her Rubber Ducky, 'Let's go pick blueberries.'"

Abby drew blueberries all around the mom's hand.

"Rubber Ducky didn't want to pick berries," Abby explained, "But his mom wanted to because they were starving. Then a fox and a wolf came along looking for food."

Abby added a square and a squiggle for those characters.

"Mommy and Rubber Ducky jumped up (Abby made the drawing jump up), but the fox and the wolf ate them anyway."

She folded the paper up small.

"Then a bear came along, and they all ate up the apple, the muffin, and the string cheese."

By that time, the picture, like the story, was a jumble of images and scribbled action that no longer made much sense.

When that story ended with a fiery feast of color, Abby drew other stories, including one that featured green peas eating purple sheep, and a blue dog that liked to cook pencils. Finally, she handed me her favorite of the lot and implored, "Will you hang this up?"

Our walls are covered with Abby's drawings. Indeed, since her work covers the walls anyway, maybe she thinks she's streamlining the process by simply drawing on walls in the first place.

Oh well. "All things will pass," my mother says. "Abby probably won't draw on her walls when she goes to college."

❋

Parenting Forever

She didn't. Well before college, Abby drew on paper, asked me to scan the images and post them on a website designed for kids. Now, for Christmas she draws wonderful picture stories for her parents and sibs that depict what each of us has been doing during the year.

Who's Obsessed with Technology?

There are fewer technoskeptics these days. Plenty of laggards won't learn to program their VCRs, microwaves, or digital watches, but few people under 50 despise technology anymore (except when it won't work), and few speak out to slow its progress. After all, it offers all kinds of information in an instant, easy email communication with everyone, and unlimited other resources in a flash.

Awesome technology is everywhere, accompanied by the promise that all our needs can be met with a capital T. Of course, most normal people don't believe that, but they wonder and worry—do I need the latest this or that; is my kid using computers too much, or too little; should I buy stock in fillintheblank.com; why can't I launch the billion dollar e-company? Or whatever. We're caught in a Technology power surge, whether we're advocates or not. It seems that everywhere politicians are pushing techno solutions; the media's pumping out stories of tomorrow's tools; and ads for new techie toys abound.

Still, there are those nagging doubts. Maybe I don't need a Palm Pilot VII, and maybe my kid doesn't need computers in kindergarten. A professor at MIT, the premier techie school, said that students can learn computing skills in one summer. A recruiter for an animation company noted that artists who've worked primarily on computer tend to show a stiffness or flatness in their work. A geological researcher said that colleagues who use computers a lot gradually grow rusty in their ability to think. (And handwriting becomes unreadable.) Even a spokesperson for Hewlett-Packard reported they hire people with collaboration skills and bright ideas over lone stars with superior computer expertise.

So what are we supposed to believe? We're surrounded by Technology solutions for the office, home, and school, and yet, even Steve Jobs, founder of the great school computer, said that Technology can't fix what's wrong in education . . . (That must have been before he said that education can't survive without it.)

Truth is, millions of people have learned to use computers outside of the classroom. I'm not suggesting that computers don't belong in school; I'm suggesting that we don't obsess about when and where our kids learn to compute. Most kids are naturally motivated to use technology because the tools and toys are fully integrated into their culture. And as prices go down, more families will have home computers. It's the older folks who still ask, why?

Well then, why? Why is Technology any more

wonderful than my coffee pot or my car?

What motivated me to become a computer advocate is its ability to simplify and enhance the writing process—in other words, word processing. As a writer and writing teacher I've always emphasized a writing process that involves drafting initial ideas, then working those into a rough draft, and then revising and revising until the result is right. Word processing makes those progressive steps easier because a total rewrite (or retype) isn't necessary, you do it all on the keyboard.

Besides writing, using a computer, in my view, fosters exploration and discovery. It supports continual acquisition of knowledge and personal growth. Using the Internet, I can enter a new world without physical boundaries. I can possess personal "property" on the www frontier, in fact, millions of homesteaders are now staking claims there, called websites. It's like owning land, only you grow information on it rather than cabins and crops, and you don't need to be wealthy or 21 to get it.

Silly, maybe, to value real estate that's nothing more than megabytes of memory. Yet it's an extension of one's mind, and resides in a place that can connect to other people and practically any resource one could want.

Unlike the early settlers of the 19th century, I can explore while sitting in a chair at home. Still, I share with those pioneers the same forward momentum and stubbornness that prods me when the directions are wrong, the system crashes, and there's no one to help. An inner light shines through, and in the end, maybe I get there, wherever there is, and it feels good.

Perhaps if we treat Technology as an adventure rather than a savior, burden, route to get rich, or tutor for our kids,

Parenting Forever

we can ignore the hype, and flourish in the big T's ability to foster personal growth. That's not obsession; it's acceptance of Technology's power. The difference is who's in control.

❉

    Reading this column two decades later, reminds me how fast and how much Technology has advanced since then. Any reader today will note that what I wrote is way out of date now.
    One other thing this column did not address is that as increasingly more students and adults began using a computer, it became a necessary tool, and being able to use one an essential skill for success in school and in many jobs. Consequently, the gap between the haves and have nots grew more divisive, and it's taken years to make Technology available to most.
    I still wonder about how much Technology is taking over our lives . . . What will be the next inventions that involve robotics, drones, self-driving cars, and all the high-tech gadgets designed for the "intelligent" house? We'll surely find out, and probably rather soon.

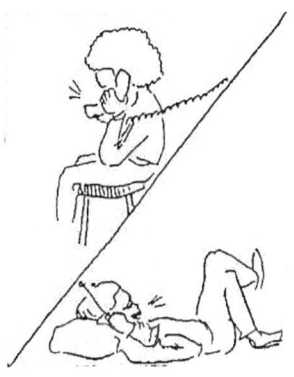

You're Really Ready to Go Steady?

Friday afternoon my daughter Molly arrives home flushed and bursting with good news. "We're going out!" she proclaims.

Oh no, not yet, I protest in silence. She only started noticing Troy last week. They've never talked on the phone, or talked much at all to my knowledge. And now they're officially linked. What are they thinking?

"Congratulations!" I hug her, beaming the public response. It's obviously too late to suggest restraint.

"How did this happen?" I can't help but ask.

"He was so cute, Mom," Molly starts to explain. "He was standing outside the team bus, kicking himself because he didn't have the nerve to ask me. So I got off the bus and went over to him. We stood around for a minute and then he finally said, 'Will out go out with me?' and I said yes. Then I had to get back on the bus."

"And that's it? That's all you said to each other?"

"We didn't have time, Mom. I had to go to track."

I try to picture this little meeting, which must have happened faster than a 200-meter sprint. Somehow, the event seems more like a movie clip than real life.

"Well, now what?" I'm really curious.

"I don't know."

I believe it. Maybe going out these days simply means two teenagers are officially interested in getting to know one another. They claim it means the same as going steady did for us, but at least we shared a few sodas and conversations before narrowing the field to one. How can Molly and Troy be committed when they hardly know each other? I wonder what chance they'll have to develop a private relationship in such a public arena. From now on, their friends will observe every little step or misstep they make along the way.

Still, I'm happy for Molly. She's never had a boyfriend before, and clearly has been wishing for it. Her older brother Justin, who had his first official girlfriend in seventh grade, teases her for delaying so long. Then he urges her to be more forward, to call guys and meet them at the movies or the mall. But I wish Justin had delayed his romantic pursuits a few years, and support Molly's more gradual development. Also, I can't resist reminding Justin that the girls he likes most are the ones who don't chase him.

So, how did this crazy attachment happen? Molly, like most teenage girls, craves a special relationship with a guy, and none of her current friends-who-are-boys fill that need. When she hears that Troy has liked her since September, she's flattered, and willing to flirt with the idea.

Then Molly's friend, Ruby, gets into the act. Ruby calls Troy and urges him to ask Molly out. Troy, who is shy with

Ready to Go Steady?

girls, finally musters the nerve to do that, and Molly helps him along by delaying the team bus.

And what happens now that they're a couple?

Nothing. It's spring vacation. They can't see each other at school and when Troy finally calls, the two of them can't figure out what to say. Ruby tries to plan a meeting at the mall, but neither can make it.

On Wednesday, Molly asks me to go dress shopping with her for the prom, and when I ask if they've talked about going yet, she mumbles, "No, but Ruby asked him if we were going, and he said yes."

"Maybe you and Troy ought to settle it before we buy a dress," I suggest.

"Well, can't we just look, Mom? We can always return it if I don't go."

So we go shopping. Molly's been wanting a prom date for so long. I figure she deserves the dress. I'll just keep the receipt.

Vacation ends. Molly and Troy face one another again at school. Molly doesn't say much when she comes home. The phone doesn't ring, and I don't ask. Tuesday, he calls, and they try to talk. Word has it they hold hands after track practice. Wednesday, he calls when she's doing homework; I don't know if she calls back. By Thursday, Molly looks haggard, and on Friday she stays home sick. He calls that night to ask how she's feeling.

On Saturday morning Molly tells me she wants to break up with Troy. "It just isn't working. We didn't get to know each other first. We don't talk. This never should have happened," the truth flies like silver bullets.

No surprise here, but I feel badly for Molly. And just as bad for Troy.

"Are you sure you want to break up?" I ask, thinking there might be a spark worth saving. "Is there a chance if you got to know him better you might like him?" I must have come across as a middle-aged marriage counselor.

"No, Mom. When I try to picture kissing Troy, it makes me sick. I just want to break it off and start all over. But not with him."

All day, she agonizes over what to say. And on Sunday afternoon, Molly finally calls Troy and blurts out her scripted farewell speech. It is kind and it is brief. Maybe Troy is also relieved when he hangs up. I sure am. It's been a major migraine day.

So, Molly's first romance ends as abruptly as it began. All their friends will know by morning. And they'll both have to explain why it's over, just as they had to explain why it started two weeks ago. That's a problem with 'going out' in this teenage culture. It's such a public event that two are like the lead characters in a TV soap opera. And how long do those relationships last?

I'm proud of Molly for being honest. For telling Troy her feelings directly, rather than through messengers. Next time, she's promised herself to get to know the guy first, before making any commitment.

Good idea.

❉

Looking back on this scene some 20 years later, I see Molly going through what so many others have before and since with a first relationship. She was lucky that hers was so quick and, though emotionally tough, relatively easy to end and learn what she wanted in a relationship.

Indeed, a year later, Molly started dating someone that Mike and I got to know and like a lot. After hanging around together at school and on weekends, they developed a close and enduring relationship.

The rituals of dating and developing relationships have changed over time, but the goal of finding someone you care about and enjoy spending time with is the same. Both our older kids passed out of the dating game and into long-term relationships, and ultimately found and married partners that are just right for them. Our youngest still has lots of time ahead to find the right forever partner.

Hurray—It's Homework Time

Back to school. Old friends. New styles. Up status. Early mornings, heaps of homework, and Mom controlling the universe when it's time to study.

But it's a new year. The teens are older, more worldly, more able to regulate their own time, and get things done. Right.

It has to be better than last year. Back then, my kids arrived home after sports at 6:30, or later, and after dinner fell asleep. Or they talked on the phone and then fell asleep.

Their teachers suggest two hours is the average time students should spend on homework every night. Justin averages 45 minutes, and Molly just a few more before her lids drop.

What remedies for these snoozing scholars would you suggest? Others who play sports seem to manage. Why is it such a problem for my kids to do their work?

Here's the problem: My kids get up at six every morning (it's a 30-45 minute commute to school each way), and for eight hours push their brains at school. Then off to pound bodies for two more hours on the field. They arrive home, eat dinner and are charged to work two more hours before falling into bed. That's a schedule that would cripple many adults, yet we demand it of kids. I feel stressed just thinking about it.

So, I'm sympathetic. And perhaps that's part of the problem. I'm supposed to assume they have Duracell minds and robotic bodies, that they can handle the schedule, and the stress. They have to. It's required. So be it.

Good study habits. That's the answer, the experts agree.

Of course, it is. If the kids establish good study habits they'll do the evening study routine without thinking about aching bodies and sagging eyelids. It's automatic: school-soccer-supper-study-sack . . .

And, the experts advise us to instill these habits early on, so the routine is in place before the job gets really tough in high school.

By all means. Around sixth grade Mike and I set out to teach our kids study habits that we knew would be useful for a lifetime, or at least through college. We read the parenting books, sought advice from teachers (probably not parents of high school kids), and planned our approach.

First, we set ground rules for school nights: no television and no phone calls during Homework Time, which was scheduled to begin an hour after dinner. We put desks and school supplies in their rooms, and encouraged them to

Homework Time

work there, in quiet privacy. We parked ourselves in the family room, suitably available if they needed help.

We even taught them study skills, like how to read or skim different materials, take notes, organize research papers, prepare for math tests, and on and on. But they forgot those lessons the instant they passed in their papers.

As homework cops, we enforced the rules by keeping the TV off, intercepting phone calls, postponing pleasures until work was completed, and staying home most evenings to police the scene and provide help.

Did it work?

Would I be grumbling if it did? I don't know what happened. Continual trampling of the infrastructure wore it out, I suppose.

Justin and Molly ended up working at the dining room table most evenings, claiming they needed our help. We went along with it because we believed they were getting extra help their overloaded teachers didn't have time to provide. But the kids became entangled in their own interactions. Justin made noises while he worked. That annoyed Molly and she made louder noises. They bickered about who had more work, whose work was harder, and who was smarter.

Now, in high school, they do study in their rooms most of the time. Probably because they each have a phone extension and a stereo too. So they have privacy, and I have no idea what's going on in there.

Sometimes, on Sunday afternoons, I arrive home to find them together in their ideal study environment. Justin's watching a baseball game on TV, chatting on the phone, and listening to a football game on the radio. On his lap is a list of history questions he answers during the commercial breaks.

Parenting Forever

In the next room, Molly's writing a paper on a computer. She joins Justin's phone conversations with flip comments that Justin relates to his girlfriend on the other end. Then Molly complains the TV noise is bothering her, and after the third protest she starts singing, same volume. Around her are pop cans, dishes, candy and gum wrappers. Justin has the same litter, but the stack is lower because he's within sight of a wastebasket and can't resist the three-point shots.

So, with questionable study habits, and parents striving to improve them, what happens next?

We try something else, of course. Since the 7:30 Homework Time failed so miserably with both teens dead tired after sports, the kids and I redesign the system. We invent an early to bed and 4:30-to-rise schedule, that actually works pretty well. They like it because it leaves them free to talk on the phone and sleep in the evenings. Getting up is hard, but with Mom serving warm mocha it's not impossible.

Naturally, no teenager in this house ever rose that early all summer, though they may have stayed up once or twice until then. And now, it's a new school year, and perhaps a new system to cope with homework that's arriving soon.

Maybe, just maybe, the teens will invent some brilliant plan to make it all happen, and I'll sit back and relax with a warm mug and a good book, how about Trig? Right.

Justin and Molly developed their own study schedules in college, got their work done, and graduated. Now they're beginning to consider how to guide their own kids through the process of creating study schedules that will enable them to get homework done. It's never easy.

First Born, Last Born, Does it Really Matter?

All but two of the first 23 astronauts in the U.S. space program were first-born or only children. Most American presidents have been first-borns. However, most inventions and discoveries have been made by later-born children. So what does this mean? Some psychologists propose that a person's birth-order position is a major influence on his or her role in the family and in life.

According to birth-order experts:

First-borns are more likely to be achievers and leaders than those who come later. They're reliable, organized, conservative, ambitious, scholarly, dominant, defensive, and serious. They may be compliant and eager to please, or strong-willed and controlling.

Middle children tend to be negotiators who avoid conflict. Middles are independent, peer oriented, team players, compromisers, socially adept, inclined to question convention, and resist rigid authority. Second-borns may compete for the first-born role, or pick a different one; later middles usually choose roles that differ from their older siblings.

The youngest is typically manipulative, precocious, gregarious, entertaining, carefree, and impatient. As adults, they often create unique positive roles for themselves.

Only children combine characteristics of first and last-borns, and may grow into one role or the other, such as ambitious leader or creative entertainer. "Onlies" tend to be highly motivated to achieve, controlling, critical of themselves and others, demanding, self-focused, and more comfortable with adults.

In my childhood family of four kids, these birth-order implications fit us about as well as our horoscopes and tarot card readings.

Some people take birth-order theory very seriously. MIT professor Frank Sulloway (*Born to Rebel*, 1996) studied families for 26 years, and his evidence thoroughly documents the influence of birth order on family role and personality.

Well then, my own family is an exception, as usual. All three of my children are biologically first-borns (two are adopted), and none clearly fit the first child role. So how does birth-order theory make sense of my family?

It turns out that birth order actually means age position in the family, which doesn't always happen by birth. Plus, factors like temperament, gender, disabilities, and spacing between children also influence personality and family role.

That makes sense. My eldest possesses the strong-willed and dominant traits of a first-born, but he's not particularly serious or scholarly. He's a better match for the last-born role—carefree, gregarious, and entertaining.

My second child is a motivated achiever who's reliable and eager to please—first-born traits. But she also avoids conflict, favors teamwork, and is socially adept—middle-child qualities. So which role is hers? In reality, the two toss that first-child role back and forth depending on the issue. Sometimes they both abandon the top spot, leaving a vacancy in the areas of conservative and organized.

Our youngest, Abby, is 12 years younger than our middle child, and fits the only-child position quite well, as she's motivated to achieve, demanding, self-critical, and self-focused. It's those attributes that have helped her grow into a karate champion, and aspire for greater success.

According to the experts, whether we realize it or not, our culture reinforces birth-order theory, and we parents have expectations for our children that fit the categories outlined above. I used to think that excluded me. But then my husband and I watched our second child win high school awards in sports we had, years earlier, imagined our first child might achieve. Meanwhile, our first was evolving from athlete to competent actor, singer, and stand-up comedian—gifts usually associated with later-born children.

It may be that expectations for first-borns are so rooted in our culture it's hard to nurture the defectors. I've learned that my job in this process is to support my kids' emerging roles, rather than define them. (Except that my husband and I expect all of our kids to go to college.)

Parenting Forever

Of course, it's not just kids' roles that influence the family dynamic. Parents' birth-order positions shape their parenting styles. For instance, my husband and I are both middle children. We're negotiators who strive to avoid conflict. Consequently, we developed amicable relationships with our kids early on, establishing flexible rules and providing boundless support. That approach worked fine for our self-regulated daughter. But the same parenting style failed with a son who needed stronger support with clearly defined limits.

Ultimately, my husband and I realized we needed to adapt our parenting style to match our kids' needs. If we had understood how our own birth-order personalities influenced our parenting practices earlier on, we might have changed more quickly and easily. Anyway, we finally did get it, and all's well that adapts well (. . . that's so middle-child . . .)

So birth-order theory turns out to be rather useful for helping us understand ourselves and our families. Unlike horoscopes and tarot cards which predict our destiny, birth-order tendencies help us recognize and revise our future. Maybe.

Looking back on birth-order theory now, I'd say that our own kids' parenting styles reflect their birth order. Our first child, Justin, is strict (and loving) with his own sons. Our second child, Molly, is also strict (and loving) with her kids, and remember, although she is our second child, she is also the first-born of her birth mother. Neither of them have the middle child's always-ready-to-negotiate approach to parenting that guided (sometimes misguided) Mike's and my parenting.

First Born, **Last Born**

Both Justin and Molly's parenting styles—however they acquired them—are proving to be successful as they both are raising terrific kids.

Scamper to the Bookshelf

Abby is only four, but her love of books and language far exceed many adults I know. Of course, I think my daughter is linguistically gifted, but the truth is she's a normal child who talks all the time and goes to sleep hugging books.

Her first word was book, and most of her favorite toys over time have been books. Abby also started talking early and one of her prime times to practice is during rest time. She doesn't sleep anymore. Instead, she hops up to her room after lunch, wearing pink doggie slippers and carrying today's favorite books. There she spends an hour reading, talking, role-playing, and singing. I hear it all over the intercom.

Of course, she also practices throughout the rest of the day, with me and anyone else who's willing to listen. A few days ago, she decided to wear her kitty costume to the market and asked me to put on face paint so she could be a "real" cat. Then I walked the aisles with a black cat in my shopping cart. Several people came over to pat the kitty and admire her whiskers.

"What's your name, kitty-cat?" was the most popular conversation starter.

Jujube was the immediate response. Then Princess, then Soapy, then Lollipop. Each inquisitor received a different answer until Abby was a cat with a dozen identities and as many life stories. When she tried thinking like a cat, purring loudly and then pouncing on the grapefruit, I decided it was time to scamper on out before she insisted on bringing home the cat chow.

I'm always looking for "teachable moments" to help Abby learn something new. Because I'm at home with her every afternoon, I figure it must be my job to help her mind grow as much as possible. She's better off with me, I reason, than at fulltime daycare. And then I feel responsible to make sure of it.

But, of course, I don't have a monopoly on teachable moments. Last week Abby came home from preschool talking about a play she was in that morning. Her teacher had the kids act out *Where the Wild Things Are*.

"I was the Mommy. Joseph was Max. And I was a Wild Thing, too."

Clearly, being both a Mom and a Wild Thing provides no contradiction for her. Maybe I should try it, too.

"You mean you told Max to go to bed without his supper?"

"Yes! And he said to let the wild rumpus begin."

I can picture my Wild Thing as clearly as I see her jumping on the couch and raging with the music at home.

That same day she also practiced making letters at school. "The letter B has two circles with a line," she told me while drawing one on paper to show me. We found the letter

B in her alphabet puzzle, and then I tried to introduce some new letters.

"This is a W." I handed it to her.

"No, it's a pretzel," she answered, feeding it to her doggie slipper.

"Here's P for pretzel," I continued.

Grabbing the P, she informed me, "This is a donut," and nibbled at the edges. Clearly not a day for learning letters. Time to put away the puzzle and dance with the sugar plums in The Nutcracker Suite.

But today we played again, and this time I told her she could keep any of the letters she knew. Most of the letters were piled in front of her before she began feeding C, for cupcakes, to her train.

Often when Mike and I read books to her, Abby stops to point out her favorite letters. When we get tired of reading, she sometimes continues on her own. She's lucky there are so many good children's books available for her generation. Her favorites don't always match her parents' pickings, but we agree on many, including *Bread and Jam for Frances*, *Mirette on the High Wire*, *Babushka's Doll*, *Owl Moon*, and so many others.

When we go to the library, she picks and I pick, and we leave with a grocery bag full that will last about as long as that much food. Maybe one day, possibly two. The moment we arrive home, she pulls them out and begins a marathon read on the couch.

Along with the literary treats, Abby also brings home books that Mike and I don't like much, like *Spot Goes to School* and *Clifford's First Halloween*. We read them a few times and then deposit them back in the grocery bag. A family tradition we started with Justin and Molly was that whenever we go to the bookstore, we buy good literature. But when we go to garage sales or the library, kids can choose whatever they want. And now we own a few that Mike or I hide whenever we can't stand them any longer. Eventually Abby finds them and guards them like treasures in her room.

So, my little genius is like every other four-year-old who's into everything, asks too many questions, and finds too many answers when asking. She's taken control of her own learning, even though her parents think they're still in charge. She reads because she loves pictures and wonders what's on the next page. And she learns letters because the shapes are interesting and because singing A is for Abby makes Mommy laugh.

Abby will probably learn to read her secret collection of junk books, and when she wins her first Pulitzer, she'll thank Spot and Clifford for keeping her company at night, long after her parents finished reading their own favorite books.

Now finishing college, Abby's book titles have evolved quite a bit. No more Spot and Clifford. Now she's reading books such as *Principles of Kinesiology* and *Buddhism and the Arts in Medieval Japan*, as well as dystopias and other fiction during vacations.

Danger Zone: Party in Progress

It must be genetic. It must be wired into human babies at birth, that when they become teenagers they will dance with danger, duck rules, and do the forbidden things only grown-ups are allowed to do. Like drinking.

Of course, my kids are different. Indeed, I convince myself they are, until the spring of my son's sophomore year. That's when Justin decides to perform in the school vocal show. Mike and I are delighted our kid wants to be involved in music, but we also know what happens when the curtain closes. Wild parties follow final performances at his school, and Justin will be there.

We find out the cast party is at the Smith's house. No drinking there. The plan is to pick Justin up at 1:30a.m. That's way past our bedtime, so Mike sets the alarm and we snooze. At 1:00a.m. Justin calls to ask if he can go to Joanne's, "All the kids are going," he reasons.

"No. Dad's coming to pick you up," I mumble, rapidly waking.

"Why can't I go?"

"Because we don't know anything about this party; because we don't want you drinking; and because Dad's on his way to pick you up." Mike rolls out of bed and trips over his clothes.

"Okay, Mom," grumble, click.

The next morning I find out about that party. Joanne's parents were away for the weekend. So, the kids drank alcohol, smoked pot, and some visited the family bedrooms. Then, because they stayed overnight rather than drive home intoxicated, they thought they were virtuous.

I'm so glad we didn't let Justin fly off to that unauthorized cast fling. And I can't understand why other parents did. Then I find out the kids told their parents they were staying "at a friend's house" overnight. The kids didn't officially lie, and their parents didn't check.

This is not uncommon. Many parents don't probe deeper into the party business because they want to avoid confrontation over curfews and drinking, and because they're afraid they can't control their teens anyway.

All this raises the ancestral hair on my back because when parents overlook such behaviors, the drugs, alcohol, and sleazy parties spread like a virus, and it becomes tougher for my own kids to stay healthy.

There are parents who don't care if their teenagers drink. It's no big deal, they chide us parent police. The kids are going to drink in college anyway, what difference does it make if they start one or two (or three or four) years earlier? These parents probably haven't read or heard of the research indicating that adolescents are at higher risk—that young bodies can't absorb alcohol or resist addiction as effectively as adults, and are less able to control urges for sex or violence.

As increasingly more of Justin's friends drink, he feels pressure to join in. "It's no fun to be the only one not drinking," he says.

Mike and I try to balance our need to protect Justin and Molly from alcohol, and the need to prepare them for complete freedom in college. Ultimately, we're trying to teach them how to handle drinking parties responsibly. We're not experts, but we think the way to do that is to offer freedom with responsibility gradually, not to look the other way while they jump into the party scene, and sink in alcohol or try to swim against the current.

For better or worse, the first step for teenagers in our family is to establish a routine that has them laying out their evening plans, then calling us about any changes (as Justin did about the unofficial cast party at Joanne's). If curfew time arrives and they're still watching a movie, we'll probably let them stay until the end. Justin and Molly know that as they win our trust, they gain more freedom.

Another step is to permit them to go to drinking parties occasionally, with the responsibility of being a "designated driver." That provides an excuse to say no, without getting coaxed or teased for not drinking. Another step is to occasionally offer beer or wine at home.

My kids are not angels, but they are learning to think about their own and others' behaviors sensibly. It won't be long before they'll be free to do what they choose in college. They'll decide whether to drink or not, when to stop if they do drink, and if they don't drink, how to have fun anyway or to exit without malice.

Years ago, they learned to cross the street safely; we no longer worry about that. We never taught them to say no to cake at birthday parties, but they have learned to stop after one, or maybe two pieces. I guess they can learn moderation at drinking parties too.

❧

I never wrote a column about it, but there was another time that Justin took on adult-like responsibility that his parents never prepared him for, and that demonstrated a keen sense of where and when urgent problems arise and how to address them . . .

One late afternoon when I was starting to prepare dinner for toddler Abby, I took out of the fridge a frozen sliced-up potato. My intention was to separate the frozen slices, so I took a knife and started stabbing at the cracks between the slices. The knife slipped and I stabbed my hand instead. Blood spurted out across the counter and kitchen wall. I called upstairs for Justin, intending for him to help me bandage the cut.

He took one look at me and the mess and called 911, instead. The medic who responded bound me up tight and said I would have to go to the emergency room for stiches. Then he turned and thanked Justin for calling, adding, "That was a very responsible thing to do, son. I hope your mother appreciates it."

Mike came home from work soon after that, and Justin stayed with Abby (feeding her a different dinner) while Mike took me for stitches. The knife had gone all the way though my hand and poked out the other side.

Who was the kid, and who was the grown-up that night?

Some Gifts Are More Precious than Presents

My mother is dying of cancer.

That's a heck of a story to write for the holidays, you say. And I thought so, too, until I thought about this season of giving and receiving, and how it fits with the give and take my family and I are experiencing right now.

Recently diagnosed with advanced Adreno-carcinoma, an aggressive and essentially untreatable cancer, my mom—who has always been remarkably healthy—now faces death. And so do we, her children and grandchildren. The morning after surgery when she asked me, "Am I okay?" I broke down like her little child. And she said, "Well, you know, I've had a wonderful life."

That was before Thanksgiving, and I thought we had little to be thankful for. Since then, I've learned a lesson or two, once again from my mother, about giving and receiving, and I have much to be thankful for.

As Christmas approaches, I am learning to give. And I thought I was a great giver—lots of presents for my kids, money to the poor, food and clothes for the homeless. Now I'm learning to offer the hardest thing in the world for me to give, myself. My own time, my work, my goals are packed away like tennis racquets, waiting for better weather.

Every day I drive to the hospital to visit my mom. I talk to her doctors, bring her family news, adjust her tubes, rub her back, read to her, whatever she wants. And every afternoon when I'm about to leave, she holds my hand and says, "Thanks, Linny." And I know I'm giving a gift more precious than anything under the tree.

The holiday season is a time of family unity, a time to share memories, meals, jostling, jokes, and to give and accept presents. Most of my extended family lives back East, and we rarely do more than trade greetings and gifts at Christmastime. This year my brothers and sister and I talk on the phone almost daily, closer than we've ever been. Thanks to Mom.

My two teens—every other year consumed by what they want for Christmas—are now wondering what they can do for Nana, to make her holiday happier. Little Abby doesn't understand what's going on, but she knows her Nana is missing at Sunday dinner, and asks, "Why?" So do I.

Together, the five of us plan how we can make my mother comfortable here, in our home, so she will not have to die in the hospital. It will take a lot of our time, our space,

Precious Gifts

our strength, maybe everything we have, except our souls, which will be so enriched. And that's the marvelous gift my mom gives all of us, even now, on the eve of her last Christmas.

We have cried this holiday season, cried until the backs of our eyes are sore. But who does not feel some degree of pain and suffering this time of year, when families come together with such compressed intensity? Discord, disappointment, unfurled dreams are as much a part of the holidays as laughter, full hearts, and full tummies. The important thing, the most critical factor in this bitter-sweet equation/occasion, is what comes after the equal sign. If the result is positive, then family gains strength, intimacy, love.

And so it is. My mother is 77 years old, and teaching us that the cycle of life is coming to a close, for her. She gave four children life, and then gave so much more, as mother and grandmother. We received it eagerly, selfishly. Now we are giving her strength and spirit to finish her journey. She receives it, with wisdom and grace.

This holiday season, as you hurry to buy and bake and beat those last minute demands, stop for a minute, and think about giving. Then give up one batch of cookies for 20 minutes of reading with your young child. Or, forget that trip to the mall to buy another gift for your husband and give him a phone-less, kid-free, candle-lit dinner instead. Give those you love a little more of you this year. Not your delicious desserts or your beautifully wrapped boxes, but you. All of you. Don't announce it, don't package it, don't explain it, just do it.

❖

Parenting Forever

My mom was the first of Mike's and my parents to leave us. Through the next decade our other parents also died, each in their own time and in their own way. All of their gifts to us endure. May we do the same for our kids.

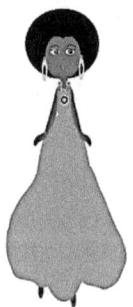 

Hairy Home Styles

My daughter Molly has been in love with long hair for as long as I can remember. The first doll she ever liked had hair below the waist, and by the time Molly was old enough to brush and braid her Barbie's hair, she was inventing new hairdos. She started styling her girlfriends' hair in grade school, and after that began fixing my hair on a regular basis. Tonight is no exception.

"Mom, can I do your hair?"

Rather than wait for an answer, Molly heads to the bathroom for her tools. Armed with brush, comb, clips, and elastics, this teenage designer tries to persuade her middle-aged mother that a glamorous transformation is possible with a new hairstyle.

Once again, I'm a captive in my own easy chair after dinner. Sometimes she creates a new form of French braids, sometimes it's a fancy twist she saw in *Seventeen* magazine. Since my hair is long, she has a million ideas for how to braid it, roll it, or wind it up and around my head. Sometimes she invents a hairdo I really like, and I wear it like that until she lobbies for a change. Then, out comes the equipment again.

One of the reasons I think Molly is so interested in hair is that she's confounded by her own. Coming from a heritage that is part African American, Molly's hair is very thick and wiry. Since no one else in the family has that heritage or hair texture, she has always viewed her own hair as different.

The real discontent began when she hit adolescence. The message she gets from Mike and me is that her halo of tight curls is beautiful. But the message from peers and the media is that long, silky hair is beautiful. She can't accept that both are true and judges her own hair as deficient.

What can we do?

Mike and I want our kids to celebrate differences: to believe that beautiful hair can be many lengths and textures, and natural (make-up free) faces are lovely, and attractive bodies come in several sizes. But our values are pitted against the images blasted on every TV, movie screen, and printed page. These media, along with trend-setting peers, are the authorities teenagers trust when it comes to physical appearance. Not parents. Whenever we try to take on these giants, the kids kindly point out our age, wrinkles, and outdated wardrobes, suggesting that we don't even qualify as judges of teenage fashion.

Beyond expressing our own opinions concerning personal appearance, and teasing them about baggy pants and bare belly-buttons, we leave fashion decisions to them. Teens use their appearance as a way to express themselves, and we think it's important to allow that relatively benign means of self-expression. Consequently, our kids are free to wear their hair and dress as they like, within a few guidelines regarding cleanliness, self-respect, and respect for others.

But Molly, the one who has always helped others achieve a variety of hairstyles, was locked into one short and fuzzy Orphan Annie style she hates. Occasionally she tries to grow her hair, but when the snarls grow too painful, she always agrees to let me cut it.

Now at 13, and still clearly unhappy with hair that is radically different from most of her peers, I reluctantly suggest she can have it straightened. She is ecstatic. She lets her hair grow for three months and I drive her in a five-inch Afro to the hair salon.

A couple hours later, when I come back to pick her up, I scan the heads in the waiting area and pass right over hers. She waves, grinning and tossing her new smooth and shiny hair. She looks so different. She looks like everyone else, and she's bursting with joy.

A couple years later, Molly's hair is still straight and quite long. She wears it differently almost every day, and continually searches the fashion magazines for new ideas.

Having her own hair to fix, however, doesn't mean she wants to work on mine any less. Indeed, my head is now the place to practice. "It doesn't matter if it looks dorky on you, Mom," she reasons, as she pulls up a handful of hair and twists it into a bun on top.

When it's finished she stands back and observes her work. "Well, you don't look glamorous or anything, Mom, but at least you're presentable."

❊

Parenting Forever

Now, some years later, I'm happy to say that Afro hair is no longer out of fashion, and long straight hair is no longer the most desirable hairstyle. Even Molly alternates between wearing hers straight and wearing it curly. I still love the Afro.

TV: Should Mom Turn it Off?

Monday morning, the house is now empty except for Abby and me. In half an hour we have to be out the door for preschool. But first, I need to take a shower and check my notes for an early interview.

Want to watch "Arthur on TV?" I ask Abby, nodding encouragement.

"No. I want to paint."

Not what I had in mind. "We can paint this afternoon, Sweetie, but right now Mommy has to take a shower. So you can watch TV."

"What am I doing?" zig-zags across my brain like a neon sign. Why am I urging my kid to watch TV instead of paint? But I know why—there are things I need to do, and the TV will keep her safely occupied.

Most mornings after breakfast when there are things to do, Abby watches TV. Right now it's not her preferred choice, but soon the television will hold her with its flashing colors, amazing action, intense crises, and quick solutions. I watched her older brother and sister fall into the trap, and now the TV is their weekend fix, their centerpiece for a Friday night gathering with friends, and their talking wall paper during the day.

"Ho hum," you who read this might say. "I'm sick of the old trash-the-TV critics who claim the box will make kids more aggressive, less smart." And then you might add evidence. "I watched a lot of TV as a kid and it didn't make me dumb or violent."

Yet the data is rising against television and I can't ignore it. Even Sesame Street is a questionable defense against the critics.

Education researcher Jane Healy in *Endangered Minds*, suggests that TV is partly to blame for the tremendous number of students today who can't stay focused, sit still, or stick with the slower-paced learning that comes from reading, solving problems, or listening to a teacher.

Why? Because TV teaches them to crave perpetual motion and to watch while others do the talking, singing, dancing, interacting, and other activities the viewers are not doing. Watching television promotes learning with more visual entertainment and less mental activity. Kids get hooked on this kind of learning and are less willing to deal with the greater effort it takes to read, write, and discuss. So now we've got learners whose minds frantically change channels when learning becomes difficult or "boring."

As for Sesame Street, Healy calls it "sensory assault." She argues that Sesame Street overemphasizes letters and numbers and underemphasizes the language and thinking skills necessary to make them meaningful.

Healy notes that if you raise kids on sweets, they

Turn the TV Off?

become addicted to them; if you raise them on TV, they also get addicted. She explains the brain is programmed to repeat experiences and that's how we learn. Consequently, if TV's passive approach to learning becomes a habit, it may put a young viewer's mental abilities at risk.

Put another way, we may spare our kids' brains if we turn off the set after one show. Yes, I vaguely remember trying that when Justin and Molly were in early elementary school. When the tube went off after one show, they went into hysterics and soon replaced the TV habit with a new one: verbal combat over which show to watch or whose turn it was to pick. It was so horrible and so revealing of what TV had reduced us to that Mike and I turned it off for a year.

Molly began reading books. Justin drew pictures and built fortresses. The result was so successful that one year extended into the next, and it was at least two years before we turned it on again.

Perhaps you're wondering why we eventually succumbed, and I'm embarrassed to admit it was kid pressure. Not so much from our kids but from their friends. Justin's friends, especially, didn't care to spend an afternoon at a house with no TV. Ultimately, we plugged it in again, though limited to non-homework days.

Abby watches a little most mornings, to keep her from creating major messes while I exercise or take a shower before my work. And now, of course, I worry about addiction and lazy learning habits.

But, if the true evil is too much TV—28 hours a week is average for preschoolers, and mine doesn't watch half that—maybe this is a solvable problem. One that even this TV-wizened brain can handle.

Parenting Forever

❉

Twenty years later, researchers are still debating the effects of excessive TV watching, as well as how much time is excessive. But in an age of non-stop media messaging along with physical inactivity, the value of escaping the TV, at least for a time, still seems like a good idea.

Bedroom Disaster

My daughter Molly is smart, kind, attractive . . . Everything about this teenager makes me proud. Except her bedroom.

When I open the door to Molly's room, if I can get it open, I face a giant tossed salad. Books, clothes, food, CD's all mixed together. This week's wardrobe surrounds her bed in little piles, Monday's shirt, jeans, and shoes to the right, Tuesday's beside that, and so forth. Between these stacks are rumpled brown bags smelling faintly of ham and apple core. Open magazines lie on the bed. The bed table's sticky with pop spilled from a fallen can, and so on. No, this is not the well-ordered mix of a tossed salad. Molly's room is the scene of a natural disaster.

So, why don't Molly's parents make her clean up the

mess? We do. We have. We will again. But why should we have to? Why doesn't Molly keep her living space inhabitable without our commanding it?

Maybe it's a question of power. Molly knows trashing her room bothers Mom and Dad big time. She can actually push us over the edge without lifting a finger. Now that's power. Sweet victory to best her own parents.

But that doesn't make sense, because Molly's the one who has to live in the rubble. Maybe she likes it that way. Can that be possible? She claims her own house will be featured in trendy magazines and she'll keep it shiny clean.

Now, our home is no photo op for *House and Garden*. There's a lot of clutter. Books and papers pile up in the study, toy cities populate the family room, and the kitchen smells of melted cheese and chocolate chip cookies. But these rooms are picked up once or twice a day. The array of stuff is organized and relatively clean. Quite different from Molly's place.

Friends advise us to leave Molly to her own messes. They say she'll change, eventually. We've tried waiting. But when Molly can't find her hiking socks and she's required to have them for a school camping trip, I have to find them or buy new ones. So I venture in there in search for socks. Even if I had been persuaded that it was Molly's personal business how she keeps her room, I then change my mind. So I begin another campaign to teach Molly to care about her room.

It's a question of self-respect, I think. If she cares about her appearance, and she does, how can she not care about the appearance of her room, and what her friends think when they see it? Maybe she gets peer status points for having the messiest room.

Bedroom Disaster?

Mike and I realize that the motivation for being neat must come from within. But since we can't find anything within Molly that will keep her room reasonable, we continue pressure from without, hoping someday she'll want it clean. Also, keeping a room clean can become a habit, can't it? Pick up often enough and ultimately do it automatically without thinking.

Sometimes there is hope. A while ago, Mike and I were away on our annual anniversary weekend, and Molly helped her grandmother take care of little Abby. Molly did a terrific job. That's no surprise—she's an unusually kind and considerate person. The big surprise was that Molly spent the last two hours cleaning house. Our kitchen was crumb-free, the family room vacuumed and even the clean clutter was out of sight. We were in heavenly shock. A million hugs assured Molly we were delighted to discover she has so much talent for cleaning.

Later that day, I descended into the reality of her room, quickly closed my eyes and retreated. One day of peace, thank you. At that moment, I thought, we're crazy to worry too much about Molly's room.

Justin's room was messy too, and later, when he was living in a house of his own, he asked Mike and I to feed his dog while he was away, and we ended up cleaning–initially by shoveling the debris into large plastic bags.

However, when both he and Molly got married, their living spaces quickly became a lot neater. Perhaps our kids organize their lives and living spaces when it finally dawns on

Parenting Forever

them that they want to, and no one is telling them to . . .

Now, quite a few years later, Abby's room is just as messy—overflowing with clothes, karate equipment, and dishes. We've stopped telling her to clean it up and, hopefully, she, too, will want to keep it neater, sometime. I think she does want to, and manages major clean-ups occasionally, but hasn't yet figured out how to keep it organized.

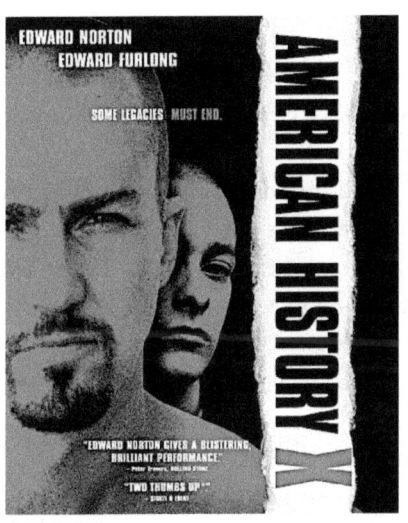

Skinheads in My Living Room

White supremacy is one of those scary nightmares I've kept in a box about the size of my television set, along with gang warfare and abject poverty. They exist, but I don't have to fear them.

Then one day Justin arrives home with a movie he wants me to see about some neo-Nazi kids. No, my son's not one of them, but his best friend highly recommended the film. So, we watch "American History X," with all its brutality, bigotry, and foul language putrefying our living room. I hardly breathe for two hours, but I can't turn it off.

The movie tells the story of a working-class White family in LA after the father is killed by a Black man. The eldest son, Derek, turns his grief to hatred against all Blacks, whom he says have been free for 130 years and still can't make it without government handouts.

Then he rants about brown "border jumpers" who fill up schools and jobs when they shouldn't even be here, and all non-Whites who have gotten work they don't deserve because of affirmative action.

Pushed by a mind-warping White supremacist adult mentor, Derek becomes the leader of a group of young skinheads. When he brutally kills two Black kids who rob his car, he is sent to prison.

There, we watch Derek gradually lose respect for skinheads, and gain respect for a Black man who shows him that color doesn't make a person good or bad, and that one can have power without violence. Derek leaves prison converted, and promptly pulls his younger brother from the racist cult. But, it's not easy to undo so much damage already done, by so much hatred spilled.

Of course, the movie actors and the audience can walk away from the problem afterwards, and all that's left is the message: skin color does not make the man (or woman). But, unfortunately, and unintentionally, the movie's racist rhetoric comes through with far more clarity and impact than the message of tolerance and equality.

We learn rather offhandedly that Derek got only three years for killing two people, while his Black friend got six years for stealing a television and accidentally dropping it on a policeman's foot. And left out of the picture is the knowledge that illegal immigrants are typically allotted the lowest paid menial labor jobs that no one else wants. Or that employers tend to hire within their own race, so without affirmative action to help them, people of color can't prove their ability to succeed at higher levels.

Skinheads in My Living Room

I won't give away the ending, but one reviewer who praised the film wrote, "See this movie and pray we are advancing as a society."

Are we? It's been a few years since Rodney King and O.J. Simpson, but only months since James Byrd was dragged to death by KKK zealots. There are too many examples. I scanned the Internet to check on the White supremacy movement and came across websites such as the White Pride Network and the Skinhead Resource Centre. I visited a few sites and found the opening remarks polite, rational, and disturbing. Further entries were downright scary: Adolf Hitler Tribute Pages, KKKomedy Central, etc.

Clearly, the White supremacy movement is alive and still twisting the minds of white folks only. Young misfits are vulnerable, particularly those angry about something connected to race—like losing to a non-White, or suffering some other slight.

After the movie, I asked Justin what he thought about the skinheads. "They sounded very smart," he began, "but they only considered one side of the issue." I waited for him to go on. Finally, he said, "In prison, Derek found out that things aren't the way he thought. The Black guy who befriended Derek taught him that people are pretty much the same no matter what color they are."

I'm happy Justin got that message, but I wonder about viewers who may already have negative feelings about race. If you decide to watch this video with your teenager, be prepared for brutal realities that emphatically bring forward serious issues.

When it's over, ask what your son or daughter thinks about Derek and other characters, and look for the influences

Parenting Forever

that have developed your child's views on race, violence and power. You may be surprised. Hopefully, happily surprised.

Twenty years later, our nation still faces racial intolerance, though other forces besides the KKK are igniting the violence. A recent presidential election season with covert and some overt appeals to racist Whites has emboldened some. Police shootings of unarmed Black men are also increasing the fear and prejudice around us. Without doubt, clear thinking and continued conversation about racial prejudice and resulting racial incidents are still urgently needed.

Readers Respond to "Skinheads in My Living Room"

I expected epithets from the Aryan race after my last column about Skinheads, but instead received support from many of you, with a few questions and comments for the record.

One reader wrote: "I was involved in a racist group for over two years. My path was very much like Derek's. The movie was very honest to me and I cried for a long time after seeing it. I just want people to know that not all skinheads are racist. If you have any questions, email me back."

I did.

He offered a personal history of skinheads which he said began in the 1960s and "was all about the working class and the little man. Race wasn't an issue, but money was and most skins didn't like rich people."

Later, racist factions emerged, he told me, and since then the media has lumped all sub-groups together.

I believe him, but I'm worried about those racist factions. From my reading of Internet websites, research articles on prejudice, and a startling piece on white supremacy in The Seattle Times (Oct. 31,1999), I worry about covert racism that appears to be growing. The article mentioned "free-agent" racists and "hate entrepreneurs" who are pushing racist doctrine over the Net. One leader interviewed said, "Today's white supremacist doesn't always wear a hooded robe, isn't a poorly educated loser and may be a highly motivated woman entering the movement because of her beliefs."

My colleagues, neighbors, friends? That's scary.

Maybe this kind of closet racism is growing because the non-White population is rising and White people are losing majority status. Some Whites are terrified of losing power, and they can't imagine sharing it.

One person wrote that racism "is creeping back up from the hiding places it took during the bright focused light of the civil rights revolution 30 years ago. The complacency and inaction of Blacks and Whites with the best intentions has allowed the forces of racism to strengthen and recover."

We see evidence of those forces following news stories with White vs. Black characters, like Rodney King, O.J. Simpson, James Byrd. The stories stir up volcanoes of racist feelings that lie below the surface until such incidents cause them to erupt. The public discourse that follows is often vicious and rarely persuades anyone to think differently.

Of course, it's a strident minority that participates in those rude outbursts. Many of you maintain that race relations have improved and continue to. One reader wrote, "I see far more reason to celebrate the progress that has been made . . . than to despair."

Yes, there are certainly more racially mixed friendships and families. More people of color have joined the middle class, entered esteemed professions and become leaders. That's significant progress, and perhaps that's another reason for the growing fear and backlash among some White Americans.

Still, one-third of African Americans remain in an urban underclass culture that perpetuates drugs, unemployment, family instability, and poor school performance. Some argue that since legal barriers to Black advancement have been removed, the responsibility for change lies within the Black community. Perhaps, but urban Blacks who try to escape the pattern are shadowed by a stereotype that is a tough rap to beat when looking for a job or any equal treatment. The research shows that discrimination still abounds.

I'm no expert on race relations and don't pretend to have any right answers. Probably there will always be some people who hate others, and acts of violence will continue to haunt the news. Still, I'm hopeful for the new millennium. While White purists rage over the Internet, there are plenty more young people artfully mixing colors so that by the time they're in charge, color slashing may be rare and insignificant.

Maybe. Whether we like it or not, the race issue is still here today. Like jammed traffic and rogue politics, we want the problem solved and off the page. But the race thing keeps coming back, and it won't disappear until we accept diversity, or until most Americans are kind of whitish-yellowish-brownish-blackish and it doesn't matter anyway.

This conversation needs to involve all of us, including people of every race, ethnicity, and economic class. In 2016, we're not talking about skinheads, but we are talking about prejudice and violence against people who look different, or act different, from ourselves. Intolerance has been present in our country since the first settlers arrived from different countries, and although sometimes we think our ideal American "melting pot" is finally beginning to blend racial differences, intolerance and violent acts appear in the news again.

Teen Hotel Party Tests Parental Trust

It came in a plain white envelope. My son brought it home in his backpack. Left it by my purse, so I'd notice, and read it. Justin's way of telling me, without telling.

An invitation issued to fellow seniors. To a birthday party for a girl turning eighteen. "A Pimps and Sluts party," it says. "No entry without Pimp/Slut attire. BYOB," plus two comments about sex. The words are framed with pictures of a Monet nude lady, large red lips, and transparent underwear.

As the mother of an invitee, my first reaction: Shock. No way will my son go. Second reaction: Shock. How can a young female of the '90s portray women as flagrant sex objects? Haven't we at least overcome that self-image?

Over the next few days, I tune into my teenagers' conversations . . . Turns out the party girl's parents are renting two hotel rooms for the event. Scheduled for Friday night, after a major exam. No adults present. Almost every senior in the school plans to attend, my son included.

So, Molly, who's an uninvited junior demands, "You're not going to let him go. Are you?"

"I don't know yet," I answer. Justin stands at the threshold. "Need to talk with him about it."

Justin edges over, hesitant, but resolved. We establish the facts. No, there will be no sex. Yes, there will be alcohol. Yes, drinkers will camp out there, not drive. Justin may, or many not stay overnight.

I am not happy with alcohol, and without adults.

But, before reacting with the parental "No," I think first this time. My son is eighteen. The very age my own friends were shipped off to kill or die in Vietnam. Old enough to vote. Old enough to be prosecuted and jailed as an adult. Surely old enough to take responsibility for his own actions. And if he chooses to drink, he won't endanger himself or anyone else by driving.

He's older, and my protective parental thinking has evolved since he was a freshman when I did all I could to prevent his attendance at drinking parties.

A year ago, I would not have considered permitting Justin to attend a party with alcohol. I assumed he'd be right in there drinking with the rest. But I was wrong. Justin seems to have identified himself primarily as a non-drinker, occasionally a modest one. He's taken on the role of caretaker for his drinking friends, and he drives them home. I'll gladly pay extra gas money to support that role.

Teen Hotel Party

In just a few months, Justin will be at college and free to join parties such as this any night of the week. Maybe it makes sense to let him practice now. With a safety net of parents only a phone call away.

I talk with my husband, who agrees with me, and decide to let Justin go. Still, the words stick in my throat, emerging as a garbled, "Oh . . . kay."

Then, of course, Molly wants to go too. I'm surprised to learn some of her friends who've been invited by seniors have their parents' permission.

"No," is the simple answer for the younger teen in this family. "When you're a senior. If you continue to grow wiser."

After the senior exam on Friday, Justin shops at Value Village for a super cheap pimp's wardrobe: Blue polka-dot shirt, checkered pants, pointed boots. A mockery of pimphood, and that's fine with me. Then he slips off to the party in another joke, our rumpled red Toyota.

At 1:00a.m., Justin calls to say the kids are acting sane and having a good time. A couple hours later, he arrives home. Safe and sober. It's a good dry run. Next year, there'll be no safety net.

At college, Justin joined a fraternity whose members drank and partied a lot, and ultimately he did too. Molly didn't join a sorority, but did drink at college though not to any extreme. Now, as adults and parents, they drink, but responsibly most of the time, I think. But, what do I know about adults who no longer live with us, don't socialize regularly with us, and don't talk about their drinking habits with us? They

Parenting Forever

haven't gotten into any trouble due to drinking, so that's good.

Mike and I don't drink much these days, and although we did when we were younger, it never amounted to much even then. People have different ideas about what's relaxing and what's fun, and if nobody gets hurt, that's good too.

Adopting Kids is a Great Way to Create a Family

The early years, before kids, were filled with books, friends, papers-to-correct, long hikes, Saturday nights, and uninterrupted conversations. Dreamy when I look back on those adult-centered years before children.

But the big dream did include kids, and finally it was time to begin making that family dream become real. However, when it was time to put away the birth-control pills and get pregnant, nothing happened. A rude joke after all those years of preventing conception. Next came the fertility pills, thermometers, charts, and scheduled sex. Oh joy. A few dates with must-do-it over our heads rendered us about as impotent as we were infertile.

Adoption was an option we began to talk about occasionally. Then often. But to adopt a healthy Caucasian infant through an agency would take ten years we were informed. A private adoption took less, but the birth mother could change her mind any time before final legalization. In an agency adoption, the birth mother signs off when the baby's released, before it's placed with an adoptive family. The risk of losing our child if the birth mother changed her mind was unbearable (we'd heard stories of birth mothers who changed their minds weeks after their babies were living with adoptive families), so we chose an agency adoption.

Already too old (31) to apply for a Caucasian infant, our options included a disabled baby, a non-White baby (American or foreign born), or an older child. Before filling out the application, Mike and I considered ourselves prejudice-free. Confronting these choices, however, forced us to face feelings about mental and physical limitations we'd never thought much about before.

After considerable inner punching and probing, we wrote on the form, "healthy infant of any race," and submitted our application. An investigation followed, with interviews and home studies. We examined our souls again and again about become a racially mixed family. Yes, we could do it. The application took a year to process. Then we waited. And we waited. It seemed like everyone else was getting or having babies, except us. Adoptive families who already had babies, got more babies, and we still had none.

Why should they get a second child, or a third, before we got our first? We couldn't understand. Not until later did we realize the agency's goal is to place a child in the best possible family for the child. Parents who already have kids, and have proven themselves able, are the safest risk. Mike and I had no living proof of our parental abilities. So we waited.

I had no fat tummy or ob/gyn appointments to remind

us we were expecting. We didn't want baby things around because waiting had become too painful. Two years, so far. That's a long pregnancy for any couple to sustain. We had no idea if it would be another two years, or three. Or four days. Our social worker could tell us nothing except to be patient.

Opportunities for international adoptions were on and off at that time. Maybe we could get a child from Korea or Guatemala. Maybe not. Once, there was a hint that a California baby due the next week might be ours. I hung by the phone every day (no answering machine in 1980). The call never came. A week later, I found out the baby had been born with multiple sclerosis. It was never offered to us, because we had applied for a healthy child. I dreamed of giving birth to that baby. Then it was snatched away and offered to a more loving mother. I could not forgive myself.

Two months later, the call came. I was in my office, talking with a student. The social worker said our baby boy had been born and we could pick him up in two days. She said he was Caucasian, but offered to us because his racial background was unclear until birth. None of that mattered. He was a healthy infant, and mine.

Justin came home 48-hours later, to a house overflowing with baby things, given and lent by friends. It all arrived instantly, magically, just like our baby. And like millions of other women past, present, and future, I was finally Mom. So ordinary, and yet so extraordinary.

❋

Parenting Forever

Two decades later, I would do it again. Having both adopted and birth children in our family is a gift. We love them equally, however they come to us.

One Plus One = Trouble

Our first was a beautiful baby. I was an attentive mother. Even more so, after the college granted me a leave of absence. And what a shift that was—from competent and respected professor, to inept mother with a first child. But like most moms, I managed to figure it out, with a lot of help.

When Justin turned one, Mike and I decided it was time to get in line at the adoption agency for our second. We didn't want just one, and we figured the long wait would put three years between our kids. Perfect.

This time, we wanted a girl. One of the perks of adoption is that you can achieve that coveted gender balance, an unusual power granted to bodies that are powerless to reproduce. So we handed in our application for "a healthy female infant of any race," and forgot about it. With Justin already filling up our lives, we certainly weren't in a hurry.

Molly arrived two weeks, not two years, later. It was a reminder of how little control we really have over this family-making process. Thirteen-month spacing, the experts agreed, could be tricky. Friends suggested it might get easier after a while, like raising twins. But it was more like raising a pit bull and a hamster. Our charming little boy developed fierce protective instincts, vigilantly defending his exclusive rights to Mommy and everything else in his universe. Molly accepted her humble rank in the family and learned to appreciate whatever she was given.

For the next ten years, Justin and Molly were worst enemies and best friends in continuing cycles. Because they competed for attention and love, they chose to develop opposite personas in the family circle.

One was loving, smart, and powerful, but lacked social skills. The other was loving, smart and cuddly, with abundant social skills.

The public bought these images, and the kids perfected them. Molly cleverly disguised her misbehaviors so no one (but her parents) noticed, and when Justin did something kind, no one (but us) noticed.

I remember one time we visited grandparents back East and Justin drew a picture specifically for grandma. When he told me his plan to give it to her, his sister overheard and moved fast. "Grandma," she summoned with a dimpled smile, "I drew this picture for you. Do you like it?" Justin quietly crumpled up his picture and threw it away.

It's true that life was tough for Molly in those days. After an episode like the one at the grandparents, Justin would probably knock her over a couple of times (which everyone noticed) or threaten one of her favorite toys. All of this would enhance his reputation as the family bully and Molly's as the innocent victim.

One + One = Trouble

Over and over, Mike and I tried to bury these labels. We chose schools and teachers we thought would help Justin behave better and Molly grow stronger. In junior high, they finally began to grow into their own, unique personalities and out of their grade-school bickers. Victim and bully behaviors began to diminish and finally left our house for good.

In high school, Molly began to see there were advantages to having a good-looking older brother, and Justin began to pay more attention to his sister's advice. They began consulting one another about clothes and other important stuff their out-of-it parents knew nothing about.

So after a dozen years, this one-year spacing started to look pretty good. Our kids had become friends. They shared school experiences, clothes, CDs, gossip, and sometimes secrets.

One Sunday afternoon, Mike and I looked around the living room and noticed it was free of kid toys, and even kids for a few hours. We were actually alone in the house. It was wonderfully quiet.

We wondered, is it possible we can finally regain control of our lives? Clearly infertile, I was already free from having to take birth control pills. We began to imagine a future with time for ourselves and our own adult friends. Mike dreamed of doing metal sculpture, and I designed the quilts of my future. A little free time, and instantly we hungered for total liberation.

Two weeks later, I discovered I was pregnant.

Parenting Forever

Looking back after all these years I have to say that after raising two kids only a year apart, it was easier for the third who had no sibling to compete with. On the other hand, she also lacked a sibling to play with, and when the elders left for college, Abby was left alone to manage, and be managed by, her parents.

HEY, MOM OR DAD! DELIVERY FOR YOU!

Pregnant at 48? Yikes!

Pregnant. Fifteen years after I was supposed to be. After all those years of infertility. It was like a gift from my fairy godmother, back from extended leave. Or was it a practical joke? I was 48 years old.

When my stomach bloated, I thought it was menopause. My doctor agreed, but gave me a pregnancy test anyway. Negative. So there were further tests, including another for pregnancy. That one was positive.

My family was stunned. Mike brought home flowers for the first time in our married life. Our adopted adolescents reacted too. Justin howled, "You and Daddy DID IT?" Molly wondered, "Aren't you too old?"

Maybe so, but maybe not. The truth is, Mike and I had wanted to make our own baby for so many years, we couldn't imagine not having it. So we went out to dinner Saturday night, by ourselves, to re-invent the rest of our lives.

That evening we did an attitude makeover. Instead of coveting the "empty nest" our peers would soon enjoy, we declared it was silly to occupy a bird house, especially an empty one. Participating in PTA took on new meaning when we realized we'd be lifers. Retirement might have to be postponed indefinitely, and we'd need to re-think everything in our lives from now until forever.

We realized our young teens were learning a powerful lesson in birth control through this experience—like what happens when you don't use it. Mike and I quit protecting ourselves years ago when we wanted a baby, and never started again when infertility proved we didn't need to. Our kids had just learned you can never be sure. They'd also get a timely reminder about how much work it is to care for a baby.

But Mike and I were not unmarried teens, and we had the resources to raise this child. So, we toasted coffee cups to the babe. My God, we finally did it. So what if we lost control of our future, once again?

As spontaneous composers of our lives together, we were at a dramatic climax.

The pregnancy was easy. We practiced natural childbirth, and when the time came, two months early, we used deep breathing and no drugs. But because the birth was so early, there were probes and meters all over my body. It was hardly natural.

But it was glorious. Horribly painful and euphoric at the same time. I felt supremely special and yet bonded to every other woman who has ever given birth. The experience was just as exhilarating and monumental as the adoption process, but different. I am so lucky to have done both.

We brought Abby into the family, just 13 years after the first one arrived, and 12 since the second. Three kids and two parents at home. Not exactly an empty nest. It was more like a full-house with three aces.

So now, Mike and I have two adopted children and one bio. Three to grow like us and also different. When you adopt kids you don't expect them to look or act like you, because they're genetically different. Watching them develop is a discovery of who they really are. When you make your own children, you can't help but look for likenesses, whether she has daddy's hair or mommy's stubborn streak.

In our family, it doesn't matter if the child is from us or others. None of them look like Mike or me, and no one acts like anybody else. A little like your family, maybe? So normal, and yet so extraordinary.

Now, so many years later, the pattern has continued . . . Three personalities fully formed, very different from each other, and from us, and yet we're bonded together into one close family.

Smoking Once, Smoking Twice . . .

My son Justin is smoking, again. I can smell it on his clothes and in my car.

It began a year ago, after he'd heard Mike and me blast tobacco makers and marketers for most of his 17 years. He still lit up.

We ranted about how cigarettes kill people. Raged about tobacco companies paying millions for teen idols to smoke in movies like "Titanic" and "Good Will Hunting." We slammed ads that make non-smoking adults look like dorks, and teens wielding cigarettes, oh, so cool.

"You're being fooled by the pushers," we told him. But he still lit up.

So we hit him with the price of cigarettes and the simple fact that Justin can't afford it. We argued that every adult smoker we know wishes he or she had never started. We threatened smoking would cripple his athletic aspirations. And finally, we threw in his face the issue of smokers' breath.

"Nobody wants to kiss a dragon mouth," we warned. But he still lit up.

His sister Molly, who drove with him to school every day after he got his license and took over the school commute, was most keenly aware of Justin's smoky habit. Once, Molly accused him of addiction, and bet $10 he couldn't abstain for a week. Justin went seven days without a single cigarette, took the money, and then lit up.

In desperation, I called his basketball coach for advice and help in pushing Justin to stop. The coach promised to apply pressure. I figured his in-your-face style would deliver impact and intimacy, so that Justin might succumb. And indeed, he did quit, again.

Longer than seven days. For a month.

Finally, wallowing in failure, I asked Justin, "Why do you smoke?"

He answered right away, "It relaxes me."

"Don't you care about all the bad things it does?" I retorted.

He shrugged his shoulders.

So I started again with the arguments, until Justin threw up his hands. "STOP!"

"You don't want me to drink, right?"

I nodded.

"Well, I have to do something!" He paced the floor. "I'm a stressful kinda guy. I need to do something with my hands. So I smoke, while other kids drink beer."

I stared at my son. "You mean smoking is a substitute for drinking?"

"Well, sometimes," he said. "But even when I do drink, I smoke too."

I began walking the floor behind him. "Can't you have a good time without either? Psyche yourself, drink espresso, or something non-alcoholic?"

"Caffeine's a drug too, Mom. And addictive." He turned and grinned at me, so sly.

Then he said, "It's like whenever I go outside, everybody's smoking. It's a social thing. And at night, when I'm driving home, it brings me down slowly, so I'm not so hyper."

I stopped walking in circles and sat down to think. Finally, I asked, "Do you want to be a smoker, Justin? Is that what you really want for yourself?"

He looked at me, at his hands, the ceiling, the floor, and into the future. "No," he said. "Not always."

I breathed again, through smoke-free lungs. But too soon. Justin went on, "I would quit now if I could. But I can't, not when everyone else is doing it too."

So Justin lit up, again. Not in front of me. Not in our house. But in the car, and with his peers, surrounded by audio and video messages that broadcast it's cool to smoke, drink, do drugs, have sex.

Weeks passed. My son bounced around like his senior classmates. Wild and free. He was accepted at college. They sent a letter asking Justin about himself, so they could match him with the right roommate. One of the questions was: Do you smoke?

Justin took two days to complete the form. Then he handed it to me and asked if I would mail it. Just before sealing the envelope, I hesitated, slowly unfolded the paper, and peeked at his answer. "No," it said.

"Yes!" I cried, and wondered when he quit. And if he would stay off this time. I was about to ask, and then stopped. Justin makes his own decisions now. Different from mine. Time to let go of that old image of who I think Justin should be. Time to stop battering his choices, and start watching what he does with them.

Justin may have stopped smoking when he entered college, but he started again, and later became an occasional smoker, and recently an almost never smoker. I think he regrets that he ever started, but he's been a lot more successful at stopping that my mom ever was. She tried many times to quit, but just couldn't do it. Justin can, and has 99% stopped. That's something.

Classroom Mothers Are My Heroes

My idea of an All-American hero is the classroom room mother. The one who chaperones second graders on a field trip to the Seattle Center. The mom who teaches art, or does science experiments with her child's classmates.

This woman must have a quick mind, shatter-proof nerves, and a valentine heart. A good teacher has these qualities too, and is worth a dozen CEOs. But the volunteer mom does it for free.

Perhaps I idolize these moms because I'm not one of them. Time isn't the problem, I simply don't have the courage or energy to survive a day of my child's antics multiplied by 25. Or the skill to engage Suzie while disengaging Sam from Freddy.

For a dozen years I taught in high school and college, always knowing my elementary school colleagues had it tougher. When I became a mother, I assumed teaching skills and love of my own kids would transfer over to helping their teachers. But after one field trip, I retreated to the home front, with smaller groups of say, two.

Since then, my help has been limited to shelving books in the library, editing school newsletters, and baking brownies.

Yes, I feel guilty. And that's what probably prompted me to say yes when asked to drive Abby and her pre-school classmates to the International Children's Festival in Seattle.

I reasoned it would be an opportunity to see how Abby interacts with her classmates and get to know some other moms. It was a chance to get over my dread of this kind of responsibility and past time to do my share.

The night before our trip, I dreamed I got lost driving to the theater, and that one of my little responsibilities refused to hold my hand crossing the street, and when I took his arm, he bit me.

I arrived at school anxious and determined to succeed. Ten minutes later, the teacher said she didn't need so many drivers. I didn't have to go. A quick conference with Abby dashed that easy escape, and off we went to the show.

I did not get lost and everyone held hands at the crosswalk. We met up with the others and arrived at the auditorium with sixty well-behaved preschoolers. As the hall filled with more and more children, I observed the faces of other moms and noticed how comfortable they seemed. I was growing tense by the second, watching exit routes disappear and the crowd expand like bubble gum.

When every seat was filled, the lights went out and the show began. Abby sat on my lap with saucer eyes. Our children were quiet as the storyteller began to play his lute-like instrument and sing in a low-pitched drone. Finally, the drummers and dancers appeared and held the kids' attention.

Classroom Mothers are My Heroes

For five minutes anyway. But then nothing new happened, other than some twitching of little bottoms on the wooden seats. The storyteller returned and continued his monologue in a language the audience could not understand and music they did not enjoy. But they were polite.

The storyteller finished, the dancers and drummers returned. And then, so did the storyteller. A few more bottoms began rocking and rolling in their seats. But they were quiet.

When the storyteller emerged for the fourth time, little Ellen spoke up. "Oh no, not him again," voicing my sentiments exactly. A few other small voices giggled in agreement. "Shh!" from a teacher silenced Ellen, but not the storyteller.

Luckily, it was over before other pre-school protesters added their voices, and before too many bored bottoms took flight.

When the curtain finally fell, we trekked to the bathrooms and headed for home. "Did you like it?" I asked one of my charges.

"No," came the honest response.

"Can we have a snack?" whined a voice from the back.

The high point of this field trip was the peanut butter cracker sandwiches I happened to bring along.

I have not signed up to be a room mother this year. But I will continue to sing praises for mothers who do. I admire your gifts, and hope you realize how much we dead-beat moms treasure you.

❋

Parenting Forever

Who knows what goes through kids' minds when they experience such events? We took Abby to a Seattle Children's Theater performance when she was 4, and when it was over the actors returned to the stage and asked the kids for questions or comments. Abby's hand shot up. When called on, she asserted, "I have a dog named Henry, and he can do tricks!" The actors just smiled and called on someone else. We said nothing.

Required Volunteer Service

My daughter's high school requires 160 hours of volunteer service for graduation. At the end of her junior year, Molly had 15 hours. What to do for the ominous 145? Like other seniors with remaining time, she could sign up for classroom helper or office assistant at school. "Bor-ing," she moaned. She could work for a local politician, as Justin did for his service, but the election's over so that's not likely.

Then her dad suggested, "Why not explore your latest career interest?" Molly had recently reported she wanted to be a psychologist and work with disabled kids.

Before that, she wanted to train monkeys. So Mike and I figured the current idea would transform into something new by next year. Especially since child care is low on Molly's interest list, let alone kids with major problems. A volunteer job with special needs children would be a perfect opportunity for Molly to try out this career possibility, and gain service credit for school. She agreed.

Mike pointed her toward the UW Experimental Education Unit, where she interviewed, and was invited to work in the summer program. That involved four weeks of hard work among a dozen 4-6 year-olds with autism, Down's syndrome, or some other disability.

In this environment, Molly would surely discover whether the career she imagined for herself was a good match, before she committed to it in college. Excellent idea, we thought, wondering what direction she'd travel next.

When Molly left for work that first morning, I wished her well and bit my lip. I would never survive the first day. I'm the one who chose college teaching because there are fewer behavior problems and tricky learning styles. I admired Molly for even attempting to tackle those issues, multiplied by extreme mental and physical challenges.

When Molly returned that first evening, I expected to see a 17 year-old refugee from Chaos. But she was smiling. "It was great, Mom. There's this little boy who's so cute. I want to bring him home."

I took a longer, deeper look at my daughter that night, and wondered what else about her I don't know yet.

The first week passed, and Molly still loved it. Every day she came home with clever ideas for handling little people, and tried them out on her sister. When Abby refused to say Thank you, Molly reacted, "When people give me things, I say Thank you, because that's how to get more nice things to hap—"

"Thank you!"

And I smiled. Thank you, too.

Required Volunteer Service

Then one day, Molly asked me, "Will you come and watch?"

I stood frozen between fear and loyalty.

"There's a little room with a special window so you can see everything. Please?"

A few days after, I drove to the school, entered the observation room, and watched fifteen children interacting with five adults. The scene was enchanting. Riveting. I expected bedlam, and found peace. I watched teachers engage little jack-in-the-box children in playful, personal learning. I saw artful interceptions of colliding bodies, and subtle distractions for those with emotional overload. I observed a classroom in slow motion. Every adult action was careful and soothing, and the kids mellowed in its graceful tempo.

I can't say that I picked up the phone the next day and offered to work there beside Molly. But, I did face my preconceived notion—my prejudice—about mental and physical disabilities. Now I see that these kids aren't as disabled by their handicaps as much as we are, when we assume they cannot succeed. With teachers like those at UW's Experimental Education Unit, and volunteers like Molly, any kids can thrive.

Now, almost 20 years later, Molly is head teacher in a classroom of young kids with disabilities within a public elementary school. She's been teaching and caring for kids with special needs ever since her experience at the UW experimental school, except for the four years she spent at college majoring in psychology. Sometimes, a thoughtful

Parenting Forever

guess and a parental nudge is all it takes to set someone off down a lifelong road.

The Daycare Divide

Recently, I read about several studies that have tried to answer the critical question for working moms: Will daycare hurt my child, or can it help? Some mothers, myself included, feel guilty putting our kids in daycare and want to be reassured that we're not bad parents for doing it. Since 70 percent of mothers now work outside the home, it's not a trivial question.

The studies conveniently ease our guilt. Almost. Their consistent message is that good daycare boosts all children's performance, and especially those at risk.

One study reports that second graders who experienced good-quality pre-school care had better language and math skills than those from mediocre centers. Children who had close relationships with their caregivers also had fewer behavior problems and better social skills. One member of the research team took the results one step further by implying that if America wants all children to be ready for school, we'd better improve their childcare experience.

The most comprehensive childcare research project to date ($10 million per year, federally funded by The National Institute of Child Health and Human Development) has followed children from birth through third grade, so far. Their findings suggest that a mother's relationship with her young child has a stronger influence than a daycare provider's. Yet the more time children spend in daycare during the first three years, the less positive their interactions are with their mothers.

The study also concludes that children in high-quality daycare show better thinking and language development than those who are cared for only by their mothers. But, full care by mothers is better than low-quality daycare.

Another study suggests that 20 hours per week serves as a turning point; children who are in daycare while their mothers' work half-time are not likely to suffer negative effects. However, more than 20 hours of care may not be as emotionally healthy for the child.

All of this may make sense. But is it really true? Sometimes I think the news articles contain selected findings that will make us feel better about working and putting our kids in other people's care.

Those of us who don't "have" to work have a bigger guilt to beat. To ease our consciences, there are other research results.

One study assures us we spend as much time with our children as at-home mothers did in the 1950s and '60s. How's that? Today's mothers enjoy less sleep, less free time, and do less housework. We're told those stay-at-home

The Daycare Divide

mothers didn't really spend as much time with their kids as the myth suggests. Instead, they spent their time doing housework (using older kids as sitters, or a playpen) and a lot of volunteer work.

Today, we leave our kids in others' care for much of the day; but according to the study, we spend all our time after work with them. One mother reported that after work she and her children are "totally together, and I'm not distracted by anything." Remarks like that make me ill. Either she "forgot" all those distractions from 5 p.m. till bedtime, or else I'm messing up on the home front . . . and the guilt hits again.

Oh well. All-in-all, I think I'm lucky to have the perfect part-time job and the perfect childcare solution. I drop my youngest off at 9:00 and pick her up at 3:00, or sometimes a little later, after her quality teachers have transformed into nurturing daycare providers.

My daughter thinks after-school care with friends is not such a bad option, at least for a little while. But, if I leave her there till 5 p.m.—I've tried that before—her day and mine quickly crumble.

There are many single mothers (and single fathers) who have to work fulltime to make ends meet; I admire your stamina. Your children—all children—deserve good care. In fact, I support extending public education to include preschool, and providing infant and after-school care for children whose parents have (or want) to work. In the long run, we all benefit.

Parenting Forever

Now, many years later, free, good-quality daycare is still not available to working parents.

As for comparing good daycare with at-home momcare, and its long-term effects on the kids, I did my own informal comparison … A very close friend of mine was a lawyer who spent long days at the office while her kids spent long days in daycare. At that time I was home with my kids and wondered which of us would, in the long run, have better adjusted kids, and whose kids would have closer relationships with their parents.

Now, so many years later, I see that there's no difference. Both of us have well-adjusted adult kids who enjoy close relationships with their parents.

My lawyer friend could afford good-quality daycare. Many working parents cannot, and yet their kids should have it, too. Providing free, good-quality daycare for parents who need it is important.

A Storm in December

It's breakfast time. The forecast here is heavy rain, with gale winds, power failures, and bitter cold. Out come our snowsuits, camp stove, and candles for a possible power outage, along with thoughts of uncooked food scavenged from a useless fridge. Strange how nature rules our lives and leaves us humbled with spoiled milk and numb fingers.

Justin just got a C on a history test, Molly's stressed by 12-hour school days, and little Abby's off on mission control—her control and nobody else's. The forecast around here is turbulent.

At 6:30, Justin is still asleep, so I go upstairs to disturb him and correct the language of his discontent. When he finally comes down I start right in, "Did you find your graphing calculator?" I know the danger of inquiry before breakfast, but Justin must learn to solve these simple mysteries. I push, "Can you remember when you last had it?"

Parenting Forever

Silence. Then he mumbles, "Maybe I left it in the library."

"Good thinking. Please check."

I'm amazed there is no thunder in this transaction. Maybe today won't be a natural disaster.

Molly appears just before departure time. "Did you wash my uniform?" she asks.

"You never asked."

She grumbles, finds sweaty #11 in her sports bag, and stuffs it back for today's game.

"You'll smell sweet," Justin jabs while packing his things.

Molly winces. "You don't always smell so sweet yourself."

"Gonna score this time?" he jabs again.

Molly slams lunch in her backpack and zips it up. "I hate you," rumbles down the stairs.

With a smirk and somber eyes, Justin zips his bag and ambles after.

"Why do you do that?" I start on him.

"Because she's my sister."

Transition time. No time for a change of weather. It's past time to get Abby. I walk into her room holding up two outfits, so she can choose one to wear. Evidently, neither one. We spend ten minutes on this, before proceeding to an equally perilous breakfast.

She finds Rice Krispies already in her bowl, and protests that she wants Fruit Loops instead. The very cereal she so convincingly condemned yesterday. What she really wants is power.

A Storm in December

"You can have Fruit Loops after you eat what's in the bowl." This is my parent strategy for the morning—shared control. Happily, it works this time, and breakfast begins.

Fruit Loops, calculators, uniforms. The morning is drenched in details. Tricky little trivia consume so much of my life it's hard to distinguish it from the important stuff, like whether a C accurately reflects Justin's learning of history, and what it means in the trajectory of his life. Or, how to treat Abby's struggle for power as a positive, exploration of her significance in the universe. If I can stay afloat today, I tell myself, I'll ponder those things tomorrow.

Meanwhile, I eat multigrain cereal while Abby spoons in overly sweet, artificially colored Fruit Loops. Why I ever let her pick that cereal at the store I don't remember.

After leaving Abby at preschool, I have to pick up a pool table for Christmas. Costco is mobbed, and I get soaked just running to the entrance. The table is so big it takes three men to cram it into my van. That's when I realize who has to unload and hide it all by herself. Talk about powerless. First the storm, then my kids, now this. No wonder Abby wants to be big. So do I.

At home, I back our van up to the garage and yank at the mammoth carton. It rips, but refuses to budge. I climb in and assault it with both legs. It moves half an inch. Then another. An hour later, the beaten carton lies on the garage floor, buried in junk so the kids won't notice.

Time to pick up Abby. The control issue arises again over snack, but this time she abdicates power, and bestows it on me.

"Mommy, I want you to make me big."

Ah, consider the twelve-year difference. Abby believes I have absolute power in the universe, and the teens believe I have none beyond these walls. Perhaps they are both right.

Later on, Justin drives home, just to be with us for half-an-hour before heading back for a play rehearsal. There is power here, but not in my limbs. There is magic on the home front that can enrich, like good fairies enable princes on perilous journeys.

"Molly scored twice before I left," Justin reports. I smile thanks for that gift.

Then, while tickling Abby with one hand, Justin reaches into his backpack with the other and pulls out the missing calculator.

Magic.

It rained today. It down-poured, and raging winds threatened. But there is power in our house, and it's warm inside. A Scarlatti piano sonata floats through the air, lifts my soul up and outward. Peace at home, and good will to all of you.

See? Parents don't have to do it all. I'm talking to you, my grown-up kids who are now responsible parents . . . Sometimes your kids will take control of the details of their lives, and they'll manage.

It still rains outside. And inside there's still magic.

Liberated Couple

My husband makes most of the money in our family, pays the bills, handles car and house maintenance, and whacks at the pricklies outside.

Inside, my life partner helps with clutter control, and might clean too, except he's too busy with all of the above, and nothing would happen anyway since he rather likes a quiet coating of dust. He reads to our youngest, plays with her on weekends, and would do more if he wasn't in New York or California, or late at the office.

I mostly battle with the housework, cook, run errands, work until school's out, and then take care of Abby.

And that's how it is around here. He and I lean toward doing what we know best, so he does mostly male stuff and I do women's work. The '60s liberated us, and this is what we choose.

My husband's different from his father and most men before the Great Feminist Revolution. My enlightened man

Parenting Forever

knows how to listen, how to talk about feelings, and how to argue without insult. To me, those things are more important than who brings home the dough and who bakes it.

The feminist movement seems to be in a funk these days because there are fewer bad guys, and because so many of its original goals have been (partially) met. Today's empowered women aren't hurting enough to fight for the remainder, such as equal pay and equal treatment, though we're continually forced to defend our reproductive rights.

As for men, the pressure to do it all has hit their gender as it did ours. My husband seems as overburdened as those early feminist supermoms, with his crammed days at work, chores at home, kid care, exercise, time for me, and not enough sleep. I watch him unravel around the edges and make the case for cutting back—at work, of course, not at home. He would, but he loves his job. And that's critical for liberated men and women.

I love my job, too, in a home office, with flextime. But I make less money, so more chores and childcare slide onto my desk and bury the book I'm writing. That's fair, I chose home over workplace when we made the move from California—where both of us had important well-paid jobs with lots of traveling—to Washington, where Mike is a fulltime professor and I can work as much, or little, as I want.

As the century turns, I suppose my husband is pretty normal. Many men are doing more housework and childcare than in the past. Many women are doing more wage-earning and somewhat less on the home front.

So . . . are wives and husbands really Liberated as we enter the 21st century? Feminists would say no, not until women are truly equal to men—same power, same pay and

Liberated Couple

professional status. But I think liberation is a state of mind, and perhaps different from complete equality. If I'm free to choose and pursue my choices without overwhelming obstacles, then I'm liberated. Equal treatment along the way is another matter, and the next logical goal.

An important goal. Indeed, I want my daughters to get a better deal. Today's working women still earn only 74 cents for every man's dollar. Women of color earn even less. We are still mistreated on the job, devalued when we take time for kids, and continually threatened by those who want to control our reproductive choices. Definitely time for that to change.

In my husband's profession, men and women are practically interchangeable. As an education researcher and professor, many of his colleagues and bosses have been women. In his field, genders are essentially equal and so are their salaries—both men and women bring home smaller paychecks than comparable experienced experts in other professions.

The same is true in my profession; both male and female writers generally aren't paid much.

But Mike and I have chosen our professions, and would choose them again. He'd also like to design and build more furniture, but is too busy with work. I'd like to work more hours, but that means mandatory after-school care for our youngest. We could use more income, but can manage with what we have. It's about choices, and we're lucky to have them.

Parenting Forever

Now in retirement, Mike and I still have choices and make decisions about the kind of lives we each want to live. We've entered another kind of freedom that's enabled by good heath (so far), sufficient savings, and a gradually expanding range of options for retired people. It may not be the promised land, but it does have a lot of promise.

So far, in retirement, Mike has taken an assortment of classes, written a book that reflects on his career as a college professor and education researcher, and completed a wide range of home projects.

Since retirement, I've written a book about the experience of falling into a coma, waking up deaf, and hearing again with a Cochlear Implant. Plus, I've made jewelry, and read many books, as well as listened to audiobooks while walking daily miles on my treadmill and the local sidewalks.

I Love the Internet!

The Internet is my esteemed servant. My personal messenger, reference librarian, as well as the information file cabinet for the universe. Other people love shopping on the Net and joining interest groups, but I love searching the Net for whatever I want to know, and discovering much more than I expected.

Besides searching the Internet, I also love sending and receiving email. This singular form of communication is informal, unobtrusive, and convenient. I can send and receive email messages when I want—not like the telephone that interrupts me when I'm eating, visiting, or otherwise busy. Without email, my sister in Maine, favorite aunt in Florida, and friends in California would be lost to the Christmas card list. We don't call each other or write letters, but we do trade e-messages, and have grown closer over the wires.

My sister and I used to talk on the phone a few times a year; now we connect almost every week. My son at college zaps me instant messages when we're both online, and then we "talk" with our keyboards. It's amazing to me that he can converse like this while watching TV, chatting on the phone, and continuing e-conversations like ours with one or two friends. Truth is, today's youth culture produces experts at simultaneous information processing, while we grownups manage one channel at a time.

Professionally, connecting with my editors, employers, and readers via email is also easier and more natural than the old form with official stationery and polished reserve. I know many of you arrive at the office and dread the daily "You've got mail" that pops up a hoard of messages pressing for answers. People who use email heavily for work are less likely to welcome great Aunt Sally's missives about her tulips sprouting in Ohio.

Another thing I love about the Internet is all those resources that allow me to search for anything from a particular movie review to the NRA's latest discourse against gun control. Sometimes it takes a few tries, like the time I was looking for information on the history of coffee breaks. I searched using the terms: research on coffee breaks, and received a world-wide collection of research conference agendas that included a coffee break in the schedule. Another time I needed information on date rape, so I typed research on date rape. My screen flashed a list of porno websites that peddle rape scenes, along with the crisis centers and sexual assault data I was looking for.

If you're not already online, or reluctant to bring the wide world home, it may be that you have concerns. Like whether the kids will go shopping with your charge card number or start searching for smutty pictures. Legitimate concerns. If you're not sure they'll comply with your rules; pick one of the software tools that will limit their access. Teach them not to give away passwords, or download unrequested files where viruses are sometimes hidden. And make sure they understand the cool kid they think they're befriending online could be older and dangerous in person.

But, there are risks in every new adventure. The Internet is worth it, at least I think so. My teenagers go online daily to do research for school, and to follow their interests in music, fashion, sports, and whatever. They also visit chat rooms where the language can get pretty gross, so my kids take their conversations to private chat rooms, or they click out.

Some people blame the Internet for promoting, or at least enabling people to spread and encourage violence, citing the vicious website of Eric Harris at Columbine High School. But that website didn't cause the 18 year-old's killing spree; it was the means of expressing his awful intentions. Indeed, his website was like a flashing neon sign, a blatant warning signal that could have prevented the tragedy if authorities had stepped in when they were informed.

The Internet is everywhere, and it isn't just a symbol or a symptom of our culture today, it is the culture. The pornography, rage, and violence right beside the latest research, oldest wisdom, and most effective help. Our best and worst right there. Wonderful for those who can distinguish trash from treasure and act appropriately.

Most of us can. So if you manage to get yourself online and discover this new world—the culture that we are and don't always recognize—use it, learn with it, and enjoy it.

※

Now, so many years later, both the advantages and the risks of the Internet have increased. Scams have become harder to detect, and terrorist groups are effectively recruiting new members, to name a couple of risks. On the positive side, Internet search engines like Google have developed into vast information providers that can instantly offer answers to almost anything you want to know.

Put a cellphone in your pocket and you have the same instant information handy anywhere you go. Plus, most cellphones have a camera that can take good-quality photos and send them to other people's cellphones or computers. And, if you want to go someplace but don't know how to get there, turn on your cellphone's GPS, enter the address, and the cellphone will direct you there.

Kindergarten Literacy Practice

My youngest is now in kindergarten. Time to learn to read, or at least begin.

"It's so exciting," I tell her. "Before long you'll be reading your books to me!"

Abby looks away. This 5 year-old speaks beyond her years, but those same words written down are daunting. She knows the sounds for letters, the simple ones anyway, like A is "ah" and B is "ba," but nothing complicated, like "sh" or "oo." Still she's pretty proud of herself, skipping around the house dropping letter sounds in every room. And when we read books together, Abby points out first letters of words and tries to guess the rest.

Parenting Forever

Yet when I attempt to show her how the first letter sound connects to the next letter sound, and the next, to make words, she slams the book shut.

Another day, I write the word CAT in big letters and show it to her, pronouncing each sound carefully, "c-ah-t," and she says it after me. Good.

Then I show her BIG and articulate each sound. She does it too. After that, I point to cat again, and she stares at it. Then walks away. "I don't want to read," she informs me. "I'm never gonna read."

"Okay, Abby," I say. "But you're old enough to learn if you want to."

"I can't." She stands defiant.

"Of course you can't now, Sweetie. Nobody knows how to read at first. It takes some time and practice to learn."

"No," she says, and goes off to find her stuffed Henry.

A few days after that, Abby sits at the table attempting to write name cards for her friends. "How do you write Susan?" she asks.

"I'll show you," I offer, and write it on a separate paper so she can copy it. "See, it says, Sssss-ooo," and then I stop. The sound for u that she's learned is "uh," not "oooo." So I fumble the pronunciation. Abby looks at me, scrunches her nose, and copies the word in silence. That's it for logic, at least with her limited phonetic skills.

So I drop it for a while. Last thing I want to be is a pushy mother.

But Abby loves to draw letters. Plain penciled ones and fancy ones with glow-in-the-dark colors. Every day she brings home papers full of letters. Sometimes words too, with pictures to help her remember. She's written RAT under a

Kindergarten Literacy Practice

furry creature with a long tail, DOG under a spotted mutt, and so many others.

Then on one of our weekly trips to the local library, I see a sign that suggests Abby can win a new book if she reads (or I read to her) 20 minutes for 20 days. I amend the rules by stating that I'll read, after she reads to me. Abby wants to win.

We pick out a pretty little book with blank pages for me to write her words, and every day she reads cat, sat, rat, and The cat sat, and then The rat sat on the hat, and so on.

Twenty days and 20 new words later, we drive to our library and beaming Abby picks out a new book. Then she wants to do it again.

A few days later, Abby asks me to write, "Come to my party." She copies it, and then writes Susan. She copies the sentence again, adding Bobby. Then Lisa.

"I'm writing invitations," she says. "I want to have a party. Okay, Mommy?"

My mouth opens to say, "Wait a second," and then shuts. I'll think about it.

That's when I realize the incredible power of words . . . they offer us independence and authority in the adult world. Maybe Abby doesn't understand the possibilities beyond this first bold sentence, but I do, and I wonder if I'm ready for it.

Words and books, it turns out, did launch Abby's future. At about 9 or 10 years-old, she started reading books about a wandering samurai in ancient Japan, which motivated her to become a samurai herself. So she started riding lessons, fencing lessons, Japanese lessons, and joined a karate dojo. Pretty soon she stopped riding and fencing, but continued Japanese and karate through college, and has become proficient in both.

How Blind is Color Blind?

My daughter Molly is part Black.

"So?" you might say, if color doesn't matter.

"How Black?" you might ask, if it does.

Not so many generations ago, $1/64^{th}$ Black would have cast Molly into slavery. Today, my daughter believes her ½ or ¼ is no big deal.

Things are different now, she says. Indeed, the worst racist experience she can remember happened at the mall when some kid whispered, "Vanilla and chocolate," as Molly walked by with her White friend.

Molly claims she and her blond boyfriend have never been harassed, disdained, or ignored. Someone did ask the boyfriend what it's like to kiss a Black girl, and Molly says they just laughed at his stupidity. No big deal.

Some would say my daughter's white-washed because she has White parents, siblings, and lives in a liberal White suburb. Still, none of that changes her skin color, which is very light, and that's what people see.

Yes, things have changed. Slavery is illegal, so is racist-inspired violence and discrimination. We're all equal now, at least that's the law. And so far, Molly hasn't faced the difference between rules and reality. She holds dear the truth of equality.

But Molly is often seen as White, and has not yet left the safety of her family and community. When she goes to college in the fall, she might discover a different truth—that not every place or person has changed. Some people will mistreat her, simply because she is (part) Black.

I recently read a student editorial from a college newspaper in Oregon. The student wrote that she thought racial discrimination was over, until she started talking seriously to other students of color. An Hispanic student was repeatedly treated rudely in local stores. An African-American's employer often "forgot" to pay her, while remembering to pay the White employees. Once, the same Black student found KKK literature all over her car. The stories continue . . . Black students stopped by police, for no violation except their color. Black students interviewed, but not hired for the good jobs. Young Black men and women, assumed to be poor, angry, and dangerous.

I read these stories, and sweat. Will Molly face such meanness? How will she handle it? We never taught her to be tough. And we never taught her how to behave if/when she

How Blind is Color Blind?

was stopped by a policeman. We raised her to believe that if she worked hard, she could succeed. We urged her to dream, and make her dreams come true. Is it possible we were wrong? Should we have prepared her for hatred, harassment, and humiliation?

Maybe Molly will escape this kind of abuse because she's light, and can "pass" as White. "No, Mom," she would say, if I suggested she slip through White walls. "I won't pretend to be something I'm not." That makes me proud. And afraid.

But Molly is not afraid. She will be herself—part White and part Black. And she will push forward the truth, the dream, that it's no big deal.

Now, years later, Molly has continued to be lucky. She received a college scholarship awarded by an African-American organization to a Black student, and has not faced discrimination at college or in the workplace. However, she works near Seattle, WA, which is definitely not like other places where discrimination still abounds and stories of police violence against Black people are almost a daily part of the news. Sadly, we still have a way to go.

Part Two:

The Emptying Nest
(1999—2002)

What Happens When Mom Tries to Cook?

I have always been a lousy cook. Disinterested and disdainful of rich sauces that seduce the taste buds, nudge the scales, and heat up the health risk.

I've tried cooking lean, but my kids won't touch it. Served vegetarian, and they picked out the beans, carrots, even the parsley flakes. Their food tastes are different and they want only what they like. In frustration, I filled the freezer with Costco entrees and microwaved a meal for each.

This year, when Justin left for college, there was one less specialized eater at home. Abby is happy with rice every night, and Mike will eat whatever I cook, so that leaves Molly, who won't eat rice, meat, vegetables, dairy, or almost anything else that's served.

"I'll eat pasta," she announced one night. "If you cook a bunch of different kinds."

So I took up the challenge.

Not just because of Molly. I had some free time. I'd just finished a novel and was waiting to hear from a literary agent—the critical link between me and a publishing contract. My hands had little to do, and they're the kind that need to be busy. On top of that, there was practically nothing I could prepare well enough to pass the pot-luck party test. So I figured it was time to learn to cook. Pasta anyway.

Instead of buying frozen pizzas at Costco, I bought *The Italian Cooking Encyclopedia*. Color pictures on every page and more engaging than my current book club novel. I read it cover to cover. Next, I roamed three markets for linguine, fusilli, rigatoni, Arborio rice, polenta, fresh basil, garlic, pine nuts, extra virgin olive oil (how can anyone or anything be an 'extra virgin'?), and more.

Within a week, I had created pastas with pesto and six other sauces. Everybody, including Molly, gobbled them up and urged me to do more. So I made fresh pizza, calzone, cheese risotto, frittata, and everything my daughter marked in the cookbook with yellow stickies.

Mike and I love Indian food (and I don't eat pasta), so that was my next journey. Another cookbook and a trip to the market for basmati rice, yogurt, and a dozen new spices, followed by thicker smells in the kitchen and stronger tastes on the table. Chicken masala, jeera rice, and spinach bharta (mainly for me, since I don't eat meat or rice).

Justin arrived home for a weekend, and after dinner remarked, "Why didn't you do this before I left for college, Mom?"

"No time then, Sweety." But now, I wished for less free time. I still hadn't heard from an agent.

When Mom Tries to Cook

The *Complete Encyclopedia of Vegetables and Vegetarian Cooking* came home with me on my latest trip to Costco. For two months I hadn't cooked the same thing twice, and this book took me along yet another culinary trail. Now, it feels more like a race track, the way I'm tearing through recipes and bumping the corners of my kitchen.

Time to slow down and mellow with the juices of my tomato quiche, and penne with mushroom sauce. The family relishes what I cook, but it seems no literary agent finds what I've made for them so tasty. My first novel is pushed aside, like the mediocre meals of my past.

But I write far better than I cook. Or so I thought. I've studied the recipes for writers, already published two non-fiction books about technology, and many articles. But the novel is received with less enthusiasm than my soggy noodles.

Now what? Mexican food? Chinese? Maybe a part-time job will keep me from mourning the buried manuscript. But when I balance low wages with daycare and high mother absenteeism, I figure it's time to chill.

Deal with the failure. That's what I tell my kids so often . . . It's okay to fail. Everybody does, sometimes. Learn to accept it, grow from it, and move on. My own advice coming back and tapping me on the shoulder. Punching me in the face. Now tickling, and laughing at me, while I remember that one failed book is only one bruised potato, and I'd better toss it out before it spoils my cooking.

Curried eggplant tonight. My family hates it, but this treat is for me. Tomorrow I'll cook again for them. Tomorrow, I'll write something spicy, the beginning of a new novel that's so delicious no agent or publisher can possibly resist.

※

After writing this, an agent did take on my book. She pitched it to several publishers, but being a complete unknown as a fiction writer, taking me on would be risky, so they didn't. Ultimately, I decided to publish it myself with BookSurge, later called CreateSpace, an Amazon company, and now two of my novels plus a mini-memoir are published and listed on Amazon.

Since then, self-publishing, with its added advantage of print-on-demand, which means the books are printed only when ordered, rather than printing a couple thousand to-be-sold (maybe) copies, has become more popular, and even traditional publishers are beginning to print their books "on demand."

Clever Child Earns an Economic Edge

"I've got a proposition for you . . ."

A male voice in the middle of the night. My son, calling from college.

"I have this great new system for studying," booms through the air waves. "I go to the Catalyst three days a week and hit the books. Works a lot better than trying to study in the dorm."

"You can concentrate in a coffee shop?" is about all I can manage in my sleep.

"Yeah. I get a double-shot mocha with a squirt of caramel, and go at it for a while."

I wait for the rest.

"The mocha costs $1.75 . . . I've figured it out, Mom, for a semester of studying, it's only 150 bucks. Don't you think it's worth investing that for good grades and all?"

Of course this is about money.

"I can't think at midnight, Sweety. Just keep studying and we'll talk about it this weekend."

Then I go back to sleep, marveling at my son's gift for creative manipulation. This time Mike and I will have to invent a response that supports study and fiscal independence.

No wonder Justin's thought about majoring in finance. He's tenaciously attentive to economic status, and clever at improving his own. Furthermore, he knows that proposals to us must be custom-designed to please academic-minded parents.

But, after 18 years of heeding frequent requests, and then watching Justin spend his own money on fast food, vacation trips, and trivia, we decided that college was the right time to make a transition. Fiscal responsibility would move from us to him.

We agreed to pay for tuition, room and board, plus textbooks and school supplies. The rest—clothes, CDs, snacks, and entertainment—would be up to him. He could easily cover it by earning money during summer vacations.

But Justin is near sighted, and the bottom line always looks fuzzy. So the first request was for laundry money. Then special soap. Then fraternity membership. Now mochas.

Dirty laundry is easier to resist than a liquid prescription for academic success. So clever of Justin to connect his coveted treat to our quintessential push to study. He has

Clever Child's Economic Edge

trouble confronting schoolwork, so naturally we want to support whatever study arrangement he can make if it works.

During the three days Mike and I have to mull it over, I take Abby with me to pick up some things at the mall.

"Will you buy me something?" That voice has a familiar ring. But I feel guilty dragging her around to do my Saturday errands. Of course she should have something for being so patient.

Stop! A different voice screams inside. You're starting the cycle all over again. So I hesitate. Mike and I have talked about giving her an allowance, and maybe now's the time to bring it up. So I explain what an allowance is and tell her she can have $1.00 per week to spend or save as she wishes.

"Okay," she agrees. "I want that purple car over there, and the doggie from the other store."

What, no mocha with caramel? I shake my head.

The solution we come up with for Justin is similar, elevated to the college level. We tell him whatever's left of the money we deposited for books and supplies can be used for other academic needs, such as study aids. When the money's used up, the rest is on you.

We're happy to support our son's effort in establishing a study routine, while holding to the original fiscal limit. Justin's happy because he gets (some) mochas.

Justin has continued to be focused on finance in adulthood, and has become a successful realtor who helps people buy and sell their houses. Plus, as he gains experience, he's getting even better and more successful. And he still drinks mochas.

How Can We Stop Youth Violence?

When the subject of youth violence comes up, my finger points at guns first. Then moves to the next tragic flaw in our society, and the next. But each failing is fiercely defended by well-articulated reasons why it is not to blame.

Guns. Our laws enable kids to commit mass murder with weapons that kill rapidly from a distance. If they couldn't get the guns, they couldn't shoot.

But: Guns don't cause kids to kill. The problem is our culture with its violent entertainment, immoral leaders, and parents who are too busy to teach values. As Lonnie Davis recently proved, if you're fixed on killing, you can do it with a knife or a garden tool. Blame the killers, not their weapons.

Entertainment: Watching and (vicariously) killing off countless people daily can dim the difference between screen life and reality. The scripted stories on TV, movies, and video games create the illusion that killing is easy, solves problems, and creates heroes.

But: Screen violence doesn't create mental instability or human killers; people who can't distinguish reality from fantasy need help. For most, the entertainment serves as an outlet for aggression, like playing or watching sports.

Culture: A culture that disdains the poor, weak, and different, while rewarding the rich and powerful, can cause hatred. A culture that lacks moral values and permits its children to grow up with little guidance, can expect tragedy.

But: All cultures have disgruntled citizens and a few extremists who commit violent acts. However, ours arms them with semi-automatic weapons, and yes, the result is tragedy.

Parents: When parents aren't home, they can't know what their kids think and feel, can't teach values, and can't provide structure in their lives.

But: Working parents can still connect with their kids, and some manage very well. The problem is parents who let their children slide without direction or discipline, whether the parents work or not.

The sad truth is that all of the above contribute to our country's avoidance of the issue, and there's no simple solution. We can pass laws that limit guns, and the gory content of what we see, hear, and read. But effective laws are likely to violate the constitutional amendments that protect the right to bear arms and freedom of speech. Maybe it's time to rethink whether those rights need further amending to fit the America we have become.

We also need to examine what causes a few of us to harbor extreme hatred, and to act it out so savagely. Some say

Stopping Youth Violence

Americans have always been violent. From Indian massacres, to black lynchings. Cowboys shooting six-guns, to street gangs and terrorists with military assault weapons. Some say it's human nature to hate. That we organize our society by pecking order with wealthy White men on top, Black women and misfits on the bottom.

I don't believe that. Yes, there are "some" who seem to pump venom rather than blood through their veins, and obsessively revile those who are different or have mistreated them.

Still, most of those avoid tragedy by venting with vicarious violence, or their fists, or with help from others. It's the one or few who plunge through the safety nets, the warning signs, and cause real grief. Then there's the killing, followed by national mourning for the dead, and ourselves, because we don't know what to do. Or, it's too hard.

Law makers are unwilling to pass laws. Tax payers are unwilling to pass money. Parents are unwilling to pass time with their kids. Gun and entertainment makers are unwilling to pass up the market. Everyone is willing to blame someone or something else, and there's nothing we can do.

Not everyone. I've heard kids raise their voices. They ask for better role models, more places to have fun, smaller schools and classes. They think stronger student government and more peer counseling would help. So would reaching out to students who don't fit in. These kids claim they do listen to parents and teachers, even if they pretend otherwise. And they want their parents present in their lives—not to add more rules, or mistrust them, but to get to know them. They want to be part of a family that cares about them.

Maybe it's time to listen to kids.

Mother-Daughter Dreams, Realities

The odds aren't great.

I'm talking about enjoying a smooth mother-daughter relationship, and specifically my daughter Molly's and mine. The odds suggest our currently clear connection may deteriorate with teenage static and greater distance.

When mothers mention teenage daughters, they often lament, "We don't talk anymore," or, "She contradicts everything I say." The familial bond that's so natural in childhood seems to fester through the teen years . . . but why?

Some suggest it's about asserting their expanding need for independence, which includes clarifying the differences between moms and daughters.

Everybody knows teenagers are cool. And their totally uncool mothers don't dress right, talk right, act right, look right, or do anything right. Yet, if mom tries to fit in, the daughter's further agitated because then mom's competition for friends and boyfriends. It seems a mother can't win.

So, how to beat the odds? My daughter and I are okay. There's little drama to our slow drifting as she navigates the teenage years. But I don't want to lose her in the fog of our silences or the little storms that arise over her messy room or unfinished homework.

It seems that too much of our communication is about her obligations, rather than her dreams. I confront her with unfinished work while wishing we could travel together harmoniously toward her adulthood.

So I resolve to find our mutual interests and spend more time together. Let's see, she loves to shop. But in stores we're like the tortoise and the hare. My child will ponder tank tops in six shops before choosing the one at the other end of the mall. And on the way back, we stop at three more, just to make sure. Me? I'll buy the first one that fits and head for home.

My daughter also loves to hike. At summer camp, she always picked the toughest three-day backpacking trips. But at home she'd rather hike through the mall with friends, followed by pizza and a four-on-the-floor overnight.

This teen is partial to anything related to beauty and fashion. She reads Seventeen and YM, spends her money on soaps and scents, polishes her fingernails almost daily, and dreams of owning designer dresses. Her passion for beautification gives me a new idea. I propose we go out for a manicure and facial. Just the two of us. A real Mother-Daughter Special. She loves the idea.

I call around to the local salons and discover the bill for both of us would total $200. My wrinkles swell like waves. But before giving up, I check prices at a local beauty school and learn we can do the whole thing for $70. Big bucks for my purse, but I sign us up.

When the day arrives and we walk into the beauty academy, I see why the price is right. The place is all wrong for relaxed conversation. It'll be like fostering intimacy at McDonald's.

The student beautician doing me is so interested in talking about her hyperactive kids that conversation with my daughter is cut to asking if her nail polish is dry. The manicures stretch over an hour, and during the facials it takes shouting back and forth to be heard. We finish our bonding experience in silence.

The most intimate part of the afternoon occurs when my teenager asks if I will get her a cup of coffee from the machine in the lobby. She's too shy to pour herself an adult drink, and I can help her out. We walk out together and she offers me sips as I drive us home.

So where do we go from here? How do I promote a closer, richer relationship with my daughter?

* * *

Some weeks have passed since our trip to the beauty academy. Since then I've learned what works for us is those unanticipated, unplanned little chats. Like the one we had driving home from soccer practice when she asked about my high school boyfriends. And another time when Mike was away and Molly came to snuggle with me under the covers and talk about nothing much.

That's the stuff that works for us. Not the scheduled "quality time" that translates into movies out and restaurant dinners, when expectations are high and so are the chances of disaster. For us, intimacy grows when we least expect it. A few precious minutes tucked into hours and afternoons together.

So I guess, my advice to myself is simply to spend time with her. And when she comes home from college this Thanksgiving, that's just what I'll do.

Many years later, our mother-daughter relationship still thrives in mainly unplanned ways and unscheduled times. She sometimes texts me, "Are you at home now? . . . Can I come by?" Or, from me, "Want to go see 'Sully' with Dad and me on Sunday? It's likely to get an Oscar nomination." The bond continues and is strengthened when we least expect it.

If it's Free, Just Say No

My daughter Molly signs me up for a "free" weekend trip . . . a surprise gift, she thinks. When our phone rings to offer the prize, a cheerful voice explains the trip includes a meeting in Tacoma and another one in Las Vegas, where my husband and I will stay in a condominium suite, just like the one we'll be pressured to buy.

Another time, Molly signs herself up to receive 10 CDs for a dollar, and later discovers she's obligated to buy 12 others that cost more than retail price. "You should have read the small print," I tell her. But I study the ad and can't find those details.

Justin calls Ticket Master and uses my VISA credit card to order Mariners' tickets for the family. Simple task. After securing seats, the voice on the other end offers 113 free issues of Sports Illustrated. My son happily complies. He doesn't hear that after those issues, a year's subscription will be charged to my VISA.

Parenting Forever

The kids don't get it, at least mine don't. They don't believe the friendly telephone voice would try to con them, and they don't ask for details. From what I've seen, today's young consumers love anything that's free, and the corporate world has discovered they're easy prey for hidden pay later.

This summer, my son hands over one of many letters offering him a credit card. A manly piece of plastic he can toss on the table to impress the girl he takes out to dinner. So he wants a VISA card, even before he has a steady job. Most of his college friends have credit cards, he says, but doesn't mention how many pay bills with 15-20 percent interest. Recently I read that over half of all young adults now carry debt from month to month on their credit cards.

Many adults do, too, because it's so easy to treat credit like free money. Overspending is epidemic in our culture, and the young in particular are easily infected. Today's kids learn to spend long before they learn to earn. And when they do earn money, they spend more. Some continue this pattern of reckless spending and rampant debt, as self-destructive as any other addiction.

Credit card companies are aggressively and successfully getting young people hooked on credit. Personal letters tempt students with, "Just write a check to yourself and receive cash. Even if expenses are piling up, getting the cash you need is easy. Take your card to an ATM machine and get some cash for a vacation."

Kids fall for this stuff, and now 70 percent of students at four-year colleges have at least one credit card, and their debts average more than $2,000.

Some critics claim that pushing plastic on campus now poses a greater threat than cigarettes and alcohol. It's as if the

If it's Free, Just Say No

Joe Camel billboard has been replaced by a flashing VISA card.

Maybe I shouldn't be surprised, given that my generation has accumulated massive debts. In addition to the national one, America has moved from being the world's largest creditor, to its largest debtor. Not a very good example for the children.

In our family, kids receive an allowance through high school, and then we (parents) pay college tuition, room & board, while they pay for everything else. That means summer jobs and some hours per week on campus, if they want fashion and fun money. My husband and I never imagined credit cards in this picture. We never taught them to Just Say No to easy money and free gifts. We assumed the shiny cards would appear after they graduated and landed jobs with salaries that afforded rent and food and car payments. After they'd learned to manage money and control impulse buying.

But here we are in a culture where greedy companies are aggressively luring kids toward financial Never-Never Land. What can we do?

My husband and I gave our teens a crash course in sucker prevention. The main message: Free gifts always come with a hitch. If an offer sounds good, ask about requirements and delayed expenses, and get it in writing. As for credit cards in college, we persuaded our son to get a debit card instead. Now he carries a handy piece of plastic, but it won't deliver cash he doesn't have in the bank, so he can't get in debt. We hope that choice buys a few safe years and a little more wisdom.

❋

Parenting Forever

The credit card game begins with vulnerable youth and continues through adulthood. We have been through several rounds of credit card counseling with our adult kids, and then advised them, once again, to replace their credit cards with debit cards, because those cards permit the holder to spend only what's deposited to the account. That way, the holder can't accrue unmanageable debt.

Now, finally, our kids have, or are beginning to develop, more responsible approaches to credit and debt. The powerful banking and commercial forces, and the lure of "easy money," certainly don't make it easy.

Beginning Computing = Advanced Frustration

My mother-in-law came to visit recently and brought along the frustration she's feeling with her relatively new iMac computer.

"Every time I turn it on there are more little spots on the screen," she says. "I think it has a bad case of acne."

The pimples, it turns out, are icons that show up every time she saves a new file.

When I advise her to drag unwanted files to the trash, she asks, "What do you mean by drag?"

She also wants to know how to empty the trash.

At this level I'm surprised my mom-in-law has successfully managed to write reports and use email regularly. And surprised by the question, "How do I start a new email message?" She's been relying on the Reply button for all correspondence.

Parenting Forever

This 83 year-old "retired" landscape architect wants to know how to use a computer, but doesn't want to spend much time learning. She has a beginners' book, but hasn't slogged through it to learn the basics.

So how does one help folks like my mother-in-law, who are in an early stage of computing and an advanced stage of frustration?

She and I spend an hour together addressing her current setbacks. I teach her how to drag unwanted files to the trash and empty it. I show her how to create new file folders and drag files into them to help organize her work.

Then we go online and do a simple search using the search engine that's on her iMac. We hunt for a CD of a theater performance by an old family friend, and then buy it online. This learner is excited now and taking notes.

In her email program, I point out the New Message button so she can initiate correspondence. We go through writing a message, addressing it, adding names to the address book, and organizing her email.

As we progress through some of the basics, I think about how grandparents and other adults without personal tutors can learn fundamental computing skills. The grandmother sitting next to me could learn everything.

I'm teaching her by working through the tutorial that's right on her iMac. Most computer have some kind of tutorial.

Another good way to learn the basics is to buy a book, like *iMac for Dummies*, or *Practical Windows Me*. But don't set it on the shelf for future reference, open it up and go through it chapter by chapter to learn the essentials of computing.

Beginning Computing Frustrations

A third way to learn is to take a course. Senior centers offer them, as do community colleges, recreation centers, and other community services. Or, go on the Internet to look for an online course.

My mother-in-law bought a computer because she wants to use it as a smart typewriter to write environmental reports. She learned to do that pretty well, but is ambivalent about the rest of computing. She wants to interact with people, not machines. Do research, but not have to learn new skills; shop online, but without advertising. Mainly, she doesn't want to "waste" time learning to compute.

Learning to use a computer is not like learning to use a microwave or a VCR. It's more like learning to play bridge or speak a new language—there's a first level of getting along, and further levels of competence and understanding. To reach the comfort level takes time and plenty of practice.

At least for grown-ups. Kids seem to pick up computing as naturally as they learned to walk and talk because computers are part of their culture, like parlor games and French lessons were a part of grandma's.

Older adults have to want to learn—not just to please the grandkids or prove they can do it, but to use a computer for their own interests or work. Adults have to face frustration, feel foolish sometimes, and persevere to become skillful and fluent.

At the end of our tutorial, my mother-in-law feels more competent and more excited about learning. We talk about continuing with tutorial software, and she asks, "Is software those disks you put in the computer's bureau drawer?"

I nod and explain that she can also download software, and when she asks what download means, I put on the coffee pot.

There's a lot of territory to cover. My mom-in-law is intelligent and able, and can certainly learn to compute. In fact, most adults can, if they're willing to take the time and to practice.

My mom-in-law didn't progress much further than this. An enduring internal resistance continually fostered her complaint that emails aren't "personal" communication, and that when emailing us she still felt "distant." And, of course, it didn't help that we lived 3,000 miles apart.

My own mom never took to computing either. But my dad loved it as the technology further enabled him to enhance his love of ham radio communication. With a computer he could "talk" in greater depth with contacts all over the world that he'd first met via ham radio.

Sweating My Way

I used to scorn people who exercise by machine. It's so—so—robotic, and so boring. Well, now I'm one of them. Mindless and mechanical maybe, but perfect for burning calories and toning flesh when it's raining and dark outside.

My husband swims, but I'd hate driving to a pool and then plunging into cold and wet, plus, share a lane with other swimmers. My kids play sports, but I'd rather sweat in private and on my own schedule. I used to jog outside, but a friend of mine who prosecutes night rovers in quantity admonished my pre-dawn ritual. At our cabin in the woods, a lurking bear or cougar threatens those jogs as well.

To be sure of daily exercise when normal hours are crammed with my youngest and work, a 4 a.m. routine is the only guarantee. Besides, those hours before the day begins are my best for pushing body and brain. I step on the treadmill, earphones pumping music, pen & paper nearby, then turn it on and start moving.

Five minutes later, and bored? No way. Ideas dance through my head at the speed of running feet. I plan the next column, plot strategies for motivating my first-grader, ponder last night's news. An hour later, I'm done. Wash up and take my notes to the kitchen for coffee and then to the computer. Before long, it's time for Mike and Abby to rise for breakfast. No wonder they avoid me when I join them with fresh ideas frothing like fresh orange juice. I'm wired, and ready to communicate. They can barely focus. Neither of them wants my routine, or my machine.

Probably the biggest complaint about exercise equipment is its curious connection to brain atrophy. Those who simply step on a treadmill or bike and push GO are at risk. They will undoubtedly face mental deceleration to low rpm's, and ultimately shut down. The legs will still move, but the brain will not. Most people step off at that point, maybe 15-20 minutes on the timer. Hardly a workout. Then they blame their brain-snoozing on the device. Wrong.

Like any moving vehicle, one must learn to drive an exercise machine. The key is knowing how to steer the mind, not the medium. Some suggestions: watch the news on TV, listen to an audiobook, or music while you plan your day, design a product, solve personal or professional problems, whatever. Just come to the machine ready for a mind-expanding experience, and then take the trip. Believe me, it works, most of the time. When it doesn't, I just pretend to think, and usually something happens.

Other hang-ups? An exercise machine looks totally uncool in the TV room where friends will see it and then eye you. So, put the aesthetically-challenged appliance in a big closet, the rec room, or beside the washer and dryer. Another negative: it's more natural to run or walk outside, and you'd rather do that. Me too, so let's go when it's light out and not raining. In Seattle? Okay, you say you'd rather exercise with friends. If you've got time to arrange it and follow through, that's great.

Your list of reasons why not could be long. Mine had a dozen entries, until I got sick of soaking-wet sneakers and safety issues, tore up the list, and bought a treadmill. That was two years ago. Except for rare sick days and power outages, my brain flies at 4 a.m. and my body craves the ride. Like my car, my computer, and my coffee pot, this machine makes the right things happen.

I still walk on my treadmill for a couple of hours every day before walking a couple more outside when it's finally light. Now, however, instead of listening to music while on my treadmill, I listen to audiobooks, and have immersed myself in some great ones, from biographies of John Adams and Thomas Jefferson to commentaries about the Supreme Court, and classic fiction such as *Sense and Sensibility* and *David Copperfield*, as well as modern fiction including *All the Light We Cannot See*.

Mike estimates that the miles I cover on my daily walks inside and outside are equivalent to circling the world every 7-8 years.

Why Do We Have Pets?

Two dogs, a hamster, nine butterflies, six river fish, two beetles, and a spider. That's enough.

My 6 year-old thinks not, and my husband's no help, just sitting there, grinning. It's me who limits the pet population in this house. And one day, Willow the dachshund played with Tommy the hamster and reduced the pet population by one. After considerable grief, my daughter realized the absence might mean space for one more pet. A kitten.

I recall our first three cats, pets of my older children now in college. Smudge regularly raked the couch; Oliver shredded my favorite sweaters; Orange Juice scaled the counter for our Thanksgiving turkey. For those, and other reasons—smelly litter, shredding fur, and sharp claws, we now have short-haired dogs who go outside.

Parenting Forever

. . . Though both of them are occasionally incontinent. Willow also barks at anything that moves, 50 yards away, outside, with the door closed. He's addicted to tennis balls, and Daisy, the mini greyhound does not smell like a flower.

My youngest never knew these dogs as puppies, and the cats went to pet heaven before she was born. She's never had an animal she can grow up with and help it learn to behave. Our aging dogs seem to her more like aunt and uncle than malleable pups.

The research says that raising pets teaches children responsibility, empathy, loyalty. Of course, I want to help my child develop these important character traits. But, everybody knows it's Mom who ends up with the cleanup. I'm the one who'll be home with the cat long after the little owner has left for college. So I'm the one who has to say yes. Even my pet-loving husband agrees. Anyway, at least I get to decide what kind of cat we get, and exert some influence over its name. How about Bug, Brat, or Bandit? All will probably apply.

What kind of cat? We've buried ourselves in library books about different breeds, and now my child can recite the characteristics of a dozen varieties.

She wants a Persian. I veto that; it must have short hair. A Sphynx? No way, it must have some hair. Siamese? Maybe, they're pretty and loyal, but loud. I pick an Abyssinian because it has short hair, a quiet voice, energy, and affection.

She concedes. Okay. Now to find a kitten. I locate breeders and nearly pass out at the price tag, $400 and up. But price should not be the deciding issue for a family member. (Did I say that?)

Before a kitten comes home, we begin training the young human who's already here. "Cats are independent,

Why Do We Have Pets?

Sweetie; it may not always want to sit on your lap, or go to bed when you do." And on and on . . .

One Friday night I spot an ad in the newspaper for Abyssinian kittens. The next afternoon we bring home a 12 week-old, reddish-brownish male we immediately name Cinnamon Toast. Poor little guy is so afraid to be away from his mummy that we let him sleep in my daughter's room to postpone meeting the two dogs.

However, the dogs have different intentions, and within an hour Willow introduces himself to the newcomer. Little Toast pops up, electrified, fur straight out and sizzling like crazy.

A week passes. The dogs live downstairs and the kitten resides upstairs behind a high fortress gate. Twice a day my son (home from college) and I bring the three together, on leashes, so they can smell each other, safely.

Daisy and Toast seem to want peace between kingdoms, but Willow plunges forward, a four-legged knight bent on battle.

Upstairs, the kitty rules. He dashes from room to room testing beds, swatting curtains, leaping for ledges, rolling over for a rub and a cuddle.

My daughter adores him. She brought his picture to school the first day and today she brought a five-inch scratch across her face. The kitty had climbed her to get to the windowsill.

No cat in your bedroom at night, I say after that. She cries while I watch the long scratch crinkle along her cheek. He'll be lonely, she pleads.

I hug her, my kitten, the one I need to protect.

Parenting Forever

Every day, while my daughter is at school, I put Willow and Toast in kennels, facing one another. Talk it up guys, I say. And they do. Then they face each other on leashes to work some more on their relationship. It may take another week; it may take a month to get them to withdraw claws and paw a treaty. They better. My daughter needs to see that pets can learn to get along, like people. They better.

Well, they did and they didn't. Willow eventually accepted Toasty, and then Toasty began to see himself as pet boss. He would stand in front of the dog/cat door they needed to pass through to get outside to their bathroom. Daisy was so afraid of Toast that she wouldn't/couldn't go out. She was miserable. Ultimately, we decided that Daisy would be a lot happier in another doting family without cats, and we found her just such a home. She's happier, but I miss her.

Monsters in Our Midst

It can't be true, I keep telling myself while reading about the cool, cruel children in Jonathan Kellerman's *Savage Spawn*. Surely those kids can be helped. Not so, argues the psychologist author. By the time they're 10 or 11, it's too late.

He's talking about budding psychopaths; the truly bad kids who mature in to impervious killers. They are cold and confident, totally void of empathy or affection—thrill seekers aiming for power and domination.

Parenting Forever

They begin to victimize early on, often torturing, killing, and mutilating animals before moving to humans. The smart ones learn kindness and sensitivity, and then play them as weaknesses to be exploited. Some are remarkably creative and some disarmingly charming until they switch, suddenly, to savages.

We are rarely, if ever, prepared for them Dr. Kellerman writes, because the psychopath's capacity for cruelty is beyond our comprehension. They're not crazy; they simply have no morals or feelings for others.

Their crimes make perfect sense, to them. He's talking about Eric Harris & Dylan Klebold, Mitchell Johnson & Andrew Golden, Kipland Kinkel, and the grown-up versions that include Ted Bundy, Jack the Ripper, and the Unabomber. We read about them and crave further information because we can't understand why they are like that. What went wrong?

This bold book offers the answer that some combination of genetic abnormality and an extremely stressful home environment may have caused moral development to go awry. Genetic possibilities include a high level of testosterone (which can boost aggression), or some irregularity in the anterior part of the brain (which can affect emotion, reasoning, and aggression). Severe abuse or abandonment can also cause a young child to switch off his nervous system in an effort to numb psychic and physical pain.

The important point is that psychopathic tendencies begin early in life, and must be countered before adolescence, when morality and behavior patterns are solidly in place. The killing kids we see in the news never got help.

What can we do? Conventional psychotherapy is useless, Dr. Kellerman notes, because it depends on a desire to change, which psychopaths don't have. Potential psychopaths can be identified, he argues, and there are techniques that can help if applied when the child is 6 or 7 or 8.

First of all, high-risk children need to be placed in a tightly structured, positive environment where punishment is infrequent and not corporal. Second, nonviolent behavior must be taught continually, by caring adults who grant rewards for success in areas such as courtesy, empathy, kindness, peaceful problem-solving, and academic achievement.

Yes, it's straight behavior modification, and Dr. Kellerman claims it works when used properly and consistently with young children, along with treatment for genetic abnormalities.

Political solutions such as banning violent entertainment will not deter psychopaths, neither will reciting The Lord's Prayer in school. Keeping assault weapons out of their hands will reduce the number of bodies, but the author contends that the most effective and cheapest solution is to identify and treat this small group of psychopathic kids. Such action can curb the rise of youth violence and diminish the number of serial killings and mass murders.

What Kellerman says makes sense, though it's hard for me to think of any children as utterly evil. Possibly because I've never met one. At least I don't think so. But the news proves they exist. I study their inscrutable faces, read of their horrible work, and see the results in bloody color. Something must be done to help kids grow up better.

There are programs that have proven effective. Yet our society is reluctant to label any kids as bad, and few dare to suggest pulling them from regular classrooms for special treatment. Fewer parents would permit it when it's their kids selected. Still, we pay for our reluctance to act with episodes like Columbine High School and all the future tragedies we have yet to know.

I don't have a specific program to suggest, or a method for identifying such lost souls. Psychologists, I believe, are working on those issues. Writing violent poems, email, and essays, or dressing in black, aren't reliable indicators by themselves. However, an accumulation of cruel and other antisocial behaviors may work to identify those who need help. And if Dr. Kellerman is right, the process needs to begin by kindergarten. I will heartily support promising intervention programs for psychopathic kids as they become available. I hope you will too.

Two decades later, as the number of mass shootings accumulates, psychopathic people in our midst continue to make their presence felt. Easy access to guns, especially automatic ones with large ammunition clips, are enabling killers to spread mayhem. It's past time to redouble our efforts to listen early and act fast.

Until Divorce Do Us Part

My mother divorced in the days when such a move was on the edge of shocking. At least that's how it seemed to us, her children, because all our friends' parents were still together. In those days, there was no such thing as "no fault" divorce—in fact, one spouse had to prove the other had committed adultery or desertion.

Who benefits from such a parting? My father, who didn't want the divorce but later made an enduring match? My mother, who left but never found the soul mate of her dreams? My brothers, who bungled through adolescence with a poor working mother and absent father? My sister, who left for college full of anger? Myself, who bounced between parents unwilling to take sides?

I was next. My divorce happened in the '70s when almost half of us who got married also got divorced, it had become so easy. Unlike my mother, who stayed through 20 years and four children, my marriage lasted just a few years with no kids. Who benefits from such a parting? Both of us were released from a major mistake, without children to suffer the split. Still, there is guilt and a sense of utter stupidity for marrying too soon and too wary. Plus, the stability of marriage as a cultural value suffers with every divorce.

Back in the '70s, grown-up flower children redesigned family relationships to promote personal satisfaction along with the belief that it's okay to leave an unhappy marriage and move on. Divorce became easy and the rates doubled. One judge has remarked, "It's easier to divorce my wife of 26 years than to fire someone I hired a week ago."

On the positive side, easier divorce laws have enabled battered women to escape dangerous marriages and other stridently mismatched couples to terminate disaster. Some, including myself, have benefitted greatly from "no fault" divorce. It's the children who suffer most.

Current divorce laws are built on the '70s belief that children are resilient and can adjust to their parents' parting. Psychologists have since observed that divorce is far more harmful to children than we used to think. Research further shows that the worst situations for kids are high-conflict marriages that last, and low-conflict marriages that don't. Seventy percent of divorces end low-conflict marriages. Those are the ones many now believe ought to be held together for the kids.

High-conflict couples are another matter. That brings us to my sister, whose marriage was clearly a mismatch, but she stuck with it until their daughter reached high school. Now the ex-couple is battling as fiercely in court as they did at home. Who benefits from such a parting? The wife, who supported his career and raised their child at the expense of her own career? The child, who's pulled and pushed from one parent to the other until she returns to boarding school? The husband, perhaps, who has remarried but bitter about losing money to his former wife. Actually, the money was only for their daughter's care, and it stopped when she left for college.

At 57, my sister has little hope of finding a full time job in her field (art history) since her quasi-professional life has been built on guest lectures, one-year grants, and occasional publications. Now she is fighting for an income, the one she would have if she'd nurtured her career instead of stayed home to care for their child.

So what do we do when marriages go bad and almost any exit looks good? Every case is different. One-size divorce definitely does not fit all. Almost everybody has tales to tell like mine, and as many opinions on the flaws of divorce laws in this country.

And remedies, ah yes, cures for divorce are abundant. Some suggest making couples with children wait several years for a divorce, as in many European countries. Others would require mandatory counseling first. Some propose that "no fault" be replaced with "hold harmless" laws, meaning the person who seeks divorce must leave the spouse and children as well off as they were before.

All of these remedies make it harder to abandon vows, but don't confront the basic issue of creating a better marriage in the first place. Of course, people have a lot to say on this topic as well, including my favorite, the three-stage marriage.

Stage one would start after the wedding, when a couple begins working out the compatibility issues that most husbands and wives confront. Divorce during this period would be relatively simple. Stage two requires a longer commitment and begins when the couple becomes pregnant. From then on, divorce would be far more difficult until stage three, when the children are grown. Then, if one spouse chooses to exit the marriage, the other must be left as well off as he or she was before.

My own daughter Molly is aghast when I tell her I was married at 23, only four years older than she is now. She thinks 26 or 27 is the right age, and I push for 30. That's how old I was when I married your father, I tell her, and we're still together, and still close.

But she wants to have kids before she's "too old," and we agree there are tradeoffs. Well, no matter what age you are, I advise, make sure you both can argue without insult and are ready for long-term and high-tolerance. I think she will. I'm hoping for no more divorce in our family.

Interestingly, Molly married at 32 and had her first child at 33. Perfect age to marry and perfect age for parenting, in my opinion.

And, yes, Mike and I are still happily together, and recently celebrated our 40th wedding anniversary.

Millennium Woman at Age Six

If Abby and I were classmates and best friends, we would both wear pink pants and t-shirts with pictures of cats. We'd choose Velcro sneakers so no one would know we can't tie our shoes yet. We would get 100 percent in spelling every week, but not math because take-away and adding columns is no fun. We'd ask our moms to pack orange cheese, Go-Gurt, and bite-size crackers in our lunches so there wouldn't be crumbs to clean up before recess. Outside, we'd all play tag and somehow Abby would manage to avoid getting caught.

My best friend would invite me to come over and join her cat club because she has a new kitten and a new cardboard clubhouse in her room. We would wear uniforms (pink pants and cat shirts) and have rules (no yelling and no letting the dogs upstairs). After we played with the kitty for a while, we'd play Crazy Bones and argue about who goes first. Abby would go first because it's her club. Then we'd eat chocolate cupcakes with tooth pick flags on top.

The club would include all her friends. No boys. Abby doesn't like boys. Except Allen. She loves Allen. No reason, she just does, but she's never getting married. She's planning to be an animal trainer. A cat trainer, actually, one who trains cats to be in the movies. She'll learn how to do that in college. And she'll make lots of money.

Money. Abby doesn't like to count it or earn it, but she does love to spend it. Last year she bought Pokémon cards and stuffed animals. This year it's Digimon cards and stuffed animals. No dolls, ever. Anything else in the toy store is a possibility, but for lack of money. Allowance is a dollar every Friday, with options to earn more. She already told all her friends she wants Digimon things for her birthday.

Abby also likes to draw and make up stories. Most movies are too scary to watch, but no tall tale that's told is too awful for her. She turns the lights off and requires complete control of the flashlight. As for drawing pictures, Abby re-illustrated the *Complete Book of Cat Breeds* in her own style, far more original that the original.

If Abby and I were best friends, she would think I'm the prettiest and I would think she is too, but we wouldn't explain why. She's a small-for-her-age first grader, with reddish-brownish kind of bendy hair, brown eyes, and a smile that pulls you in and holds you for infinity. She laughs a lot and talks a lot. Too much, maybe. Other kids at her lunch table ask her to be quiet, but she has to tell every detail about the fish at the aquarium and the poisonous snakes on Amazing Animals. That's her favorite TV show, or it was until she discovered Digimon.

Millennium Woman at Age Six

When Abby comes to my house she wants to do computer games, but I want to play with Barbies. So I set up a house and start to play, while she digs through my old toys and pretty soon we're inventing some other game.

Did I mention Brownie Scouts? I joined a while ago, and so Abby wanted to join too. At one meeting we got special sheets of paper to write down our good deeds. Her list reads: Helped Mom clear dishes off the table; found the cat; carried a grocery bag from the car; asked mom if she had a nice day; set the table . . . Abby has five good deeds so far. We need twenty by Thursday.

My friend doesn't worry about much. But she sometimes worries about nightmares, big dogs, polluted rivers, lost rain forests, and animals becoming extinct. Abby doesn't eat McDonald's hamburgers because somebody told her that someone said the company treats its cattle badly. Or maybe it was Burger King. She doesn't like hamburgers anyway.

Speaking of food, Abby wants very much to help hungry people. She'll give them all her McDonald's Happy Meal hamburgers, if she can keep the toys. She also likes to deposit change from her mom's purse into the little donation boxes at the grocery store checkout. Abby would give away her allowance, too, except then she'd have nothing to spend.

The worst thing in the world is a bad fire, she says, and the best thing is her cat Toasty. Well, maybe her mom and dad, sister and brother come first. Then the cat.

This millennium six-year-old is but a moment in time, passing as swiftly as days and months, from Pokémon to Crazy Bones and cats, through adolescence and adulthood as the century grows up and TV programs change and fashions disappear. She is who we are but never will become . . . none of us, and every one of us.

Kids on Computers: When is it Too Soon?

My son started computing at age 4. I started at 30. My mother-in-law started at 81. We're all still learning.

But the issue is currently being debated: When should today's kids begin computing?

Some parents believe that learning to use computers at an early age will help children be smarter and better prepared. Others think that 3, 4, 5, even 6 years-old is too young.

Not only parents, but also many educators, psychologists, and physicans are sharply divided on the issue.

There is no easy answer. Examining arguments on both sides could cast light on the choices you may be facing.

Firmly grounded in the belief that children should begin computing in preschool is the International Society for Technology in Education (NETS), which extablished the national Educational Technology Standards project to develop standards for the use of technology in schools.

The NETS project has developed Profiles for Technology Literate Students to guide technology curriculm so that students are proficient with computer skills by the time they graduate from high school.

Because computers are increasingly more prominent in schools, educators may find it helpful to have guides such as the profiles to provide some measure of what's appropriate and expected at each grade level.

Still, some raise their eyebrows when it comes to preschool children. Even if 4 year-olds can learn to use a mouse and draw pictures on a screen, is it really such a good idea?

The Alliance for Children, would answer with a resounding No. They believe that computers should play a minor role or no role at all in elementary school.

The Alliance can cite evidence of behavioral changes in today's children indicating that kids' increased time with technology may be related to a noticeable increase in hyperactivity and depression. Also, young children in different stages of brain development have particular needs that technology can't meet.

Others argue that it's become fashionable to bring young children into the adult world too soon, shrinking the stages of childhood and preventing them from completing necessary developmental tasks.

For example, kids don't need technological expertise to enter school successfully. Instead, they should be able to express themselves, listen and follow directions, complete a task before starting another and cooperate with older children.

Interestingly, the Experimental Education Unit at the University of Washington uses the computer to promote social interaction among young children. Professor Schwartz explains that the computer is particularly effective in helping autistic kids develop skills in communication and social interaction. "The children work in pairs, which means they have to negotiate turns, sit close to someone, and play an interactive game," she says. "They're really motivated to play, and the interaction helps their social skills."

Schwartz believes the computer is neither good nor bad; it all depends on how it's used. "I've seen parents who sit their kids on their laps and play computer games with them. This can't be bad," she says. "But if you leave a 2 year-old alone in front of a computer, it's about the same as leaving him in front of a TV. Not so good."

However, using the computer as a baby-sitter is becoming more common, and the number of hours children sit in front of computer screens, or the TV, of course, appears to be going up.

So what do we do? Embrace electronic learning and begin teaching children to be intelligent viewers and computer users at an early age? Or postpone their computer education until they've at least learned to talk, read, and tie their shoes?

The recommendation to postpone computer use in schools until grade three (with exceptions for particular situations), and limit computer use without total abstinence at home sounds reasonable. And it leaves room to respond to my child's interests.

My first child loved computers at 4, so I supported his infatuation, with controls. The next child wasn't interested at all until junior high, and I didn't push. She turned on to computers around eighth grade and caught up to her brother in high school.

Parenting Forever

The youngest, who's almost 7, hadn't shown any interest until a few months ago when she discovered Jump Start Second Grade from Knowledge Adventure. Now I limit her screen time, balancing fast-paced animations with slower-paced art projects and family reading. I have to be vigilant, though, for flashing screens have a way of edging out everything else.

In fact, the more relevant issue for today's children is what to do when they're really fired up. That answer is the same as for most things in education and in life: go for balance.

Now, years later, balance is what most people now agree is the best way to view the use of computer technology in school. Less in elementary school, more in middle school, and even more in high school. By the time students reach high school they definitely need basic computer skills, and a higher level of competence is better. Still, balance is the goal, though the emphasis shifts toward acquiring expertise as students get older.

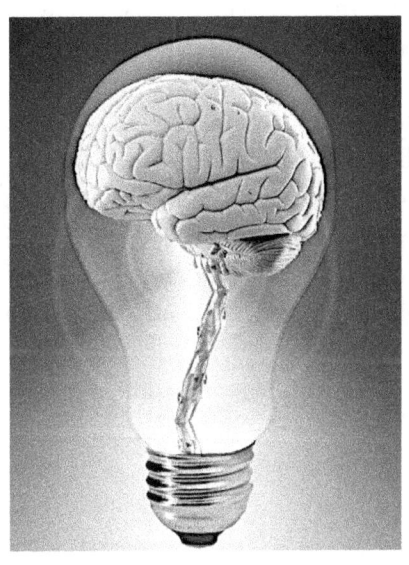

Thinking on the Surface, and Thinking Deep

Are we becoming a nation of hurried, shallow thinkers? Do we choose magazine articles over books, summaries of expert opinions over studying the issues ourselves? What books do we really read besides how-to's and Harry Potter?

Recently I've been talking to colleagues who believe American's immersion in TV and computer technologies is changing our culture. They say our appetite for sound bites and text bits promotes a kind of "information grazing" that leads to dumbing down of people's ability to think deeply.

Few people these days are willing to put sustained effort into reading and thinking about a serious work of literature, for example.

Book clubs exist because some of us still value this kind of endeavor, but most bookish members are over 40, and the greatest push for change is coming from the emerging majority—our kids and grandkids.

My colleagues maintain there's a cultural shift in how we think about information and how we process it. They say we're moving away from the sort of thinking that traditional book-based culture fostered—the slower, analytical, read the book, think about it, and discuss it approach.

Difficult, detail-packed tomes require hours of concentration, and we as a culture don't value that anymore, my colleagues argue. They say we're adopting a more condensed way of dealing with the world that's faster, more compressed, less complete.

But, does this mean we're shallow thinkers?

I'm not convinced. I wonder if it's essential to read lengthy texts to prompt deep thinking. Seems to me if the ideas are worthy, length is irrelevant. My colleagues argue if the ideas are worthy, it takes time to lay out the complexities that surround them. Ah.

I suppose this article feeds their fears—it's short, presents the ideas without intellectual back-up, and you're reading it.

Truth is, I am trying to think analytically about this issue, discussing it with a historian, sociologist, and a technology expert, and attempting to draw logic and meaning out of their arguments. However, I've barely dipped into the related books my colleagues have suggested—I keep falling asleep.

Alas, I'm a shallow thinker. I like articles, excerpts, video clips, and the Internet. Oh my gosh, I must be hopeless.

But wait a minute, I also read classics, some research studies, and other dense volumes; maybe I'm not so hopeless.

Now there appears to be a contradiction in my argument—some weighty books I'll read, and others I won't?

Maybe the issue isn't as simple as great books are good, and Web pages are bad. And maybe our intellectual lives aren't deteriorating even though they may be changing. Searching the Internet for information does enable us to gather information from many different sources with different points-of-view, more than reading a few big tomes would provide. The trick for us Web readers is making sure we check the validity/respectability of the sources we read.

And if deep thinking is the issue here, let's look at it without pointing fingers at today's information resources and fast-paced living. If the goal is to think analytically about a topic, clearly one way is to study a book written by a deep thinker and discuss its ideas with others. Perhaps another way is to collect information on the topic written by several different experts and compare summaries of their work.

Suppose I want to learn about Sigmund Freud. Why should I study his own volumes in great depth when I can read excerpts and synopses and cover other experts' analyses of Freud's ideas at the same time? Especially since there are many experts in his area who vehemently disagree with his ideas.

My esteemed colleagues would argue this sacrifices depth for breadth.

Parenting Forever

I argue it's as worthy to look at how different experts approach a topic as it is to spend my time studying one perspective more deeply.

They would say it's important to study those other perspectives in depth too.

I say that's unrealistic. I don't have time.

They would say that's right; the culture is changing.

Well, maybe so. But that doesn't mean our thinking is impaired just because our methods of doing it are different.

Finally, I'll add that perhaps it's best to leave deep study and deep analysis of Freud, for instance, to academics and those studying to become psychologists and psychiatrists.

Or, leave the deep study and analysis till retirement, my husband suggests. And he reminds me that my car's license plate now says: READER.

I suggest back to him that he can study Freud in retirement. I'll read novels.

We Pulled the Plug

Flashback to when the two older kids were much younger, like around 9 and 10 . . .

It was almost TV time. Justin and Molly were squabbling about what show they would watch when the clock struck 5:00 and they raced to the set. ***///###??? Screen litter.

They howled.

The cable company reported it would take hours to fix.

I watched my kids' inability to cope, and flashed back to all those articles I'd read about the harmful effects of TV, and children's dependence on it.

That night my husband and I talked, and planned.

The next day, when the kids came home from school, they found art materials, books, and games where the TV used to be.

I tried to give them my "TV isn't good for you" speech, including "Over 3,000 studies show a direct connection between TV watching and aggression." They squawked. So I just said, "It's clear that you've become addicted to the television, so your dad and I decided to put it away for a while." The rest of that afternoon was a disaster.

The next day Molly grabbed a book and retreated to her bedroom. Justin paced the room where the TV wasn't and attempted to debate the case. "The TV teaches us stuff, like about wild animals and how to play sports," he began.

"You don't watch animal shows anymore," I reminded him, and pointed to an article. "This says by the time you're in junior high you'll have seen more than 8,000 murders and 10,000 other violent acts on TV." I pointed to another article, but then decided not to mention that a typical teenager views nearly 14,000 sexual encounters on television every year, and most of them outside the value system we're trying to convey.

"How about if I only watch sports?" he pleaded.

"Sweety," I began, "Dad and I don't like what TV is doing to you and your sister. You don't make things anymore; you don't read or play games, and sometimes you even talk fresh and act hyper." The trial went on for over an hour. The television stayed in the garage.

The next day Justin drew monster pictures and Molly kept reading. By the end of the week, she'd finished two books. By the end of the month, his drawings evolved from blood & gore, to animals and sports heroes.

Life was harder for me, helping them imagine what to do with the time. I made lists of suggestions, and I played games, caught balls, and acted as playmate when there was no other. When friends came over, I was free, but their friends (mostly his) wanted to watch television. When my kids went to other houses, they watched. Justin began going to his friends more often because without a TV, he said, they don't want to come here.

A year passed. Molly read dozens of books. Justin spent his afternoons at other kids' houses. My husband and I worried about what he was watching. R-rated movies, we found out, and one or two X's that were hidden in a master bedroom.

What to do? My kids were almost in middle school by then, and their culture (especially his) was saturated with TV and video games. We refused to buy a video game machine after observing that most of the games were violent. But, the kid culture was growing more important in their lives. The higher we built our fortress, the more isolated they felt.

Finally, Justin, who had never managed to save an allowance in his life, banked enough to buy a Nintendo. We said yes. Friends trickled in to play with the great warring machine. But there was still no TV, their resting place between battles.

Then Molly went to a friend's house and watched a video about a girl who was drugged at a party, passed out, and raped by a boy with AIDS. I was furious. Partly because the parent allowed my daughter to watch the movie without my permission, and partly because I wanted to be there to talk with Molly about what happened.

Time for another critical conversation with my husband. Our kids were watching and forming opinions about sex, drugs, and violence without us. Ultimately, we decided to bring the TV back into our house and begin helping them learn how to critically process what they see.

Indeed, television quickly slipped back into their lives, and now when they come home from college, the TV glows in the corner until they leave again. When their little sister Abby wanders into the room with the flashing screen, they tell her to find something better to do, because "the TV will rot your brain."

The youngest runs out of the room to save herself, and later asks one of them, "Is your brain rotten?"

Now, some years later, we haven't seen any signs of brain rot. Even though . . .

A TV is constantly on in Justin's house, and his family gathers around to watch sports in the evenings or favorite shows, and catch some news while eating breakfast in the morning. Otherwise, it's ignored as they pass through to other places and adventures.

The TV is on in Molly's house when favorite teams or shows are playing, and also for news. And possibly other times, too, until somebody turns it off.

Abby is still at college, so she's pretty busy in the evenings, though does find time to watch favorite shows and streamed movies.

All three are more closely glued to another screen—the 2x4-inch window on the world that their iPhones provide.

Generation Gaps and Bridges

Three generations rocked and reviewed lifestyles at our house over the first holiday this season . . .

Picture a 7 year-old girl in a black beret armed with a fat yellow Pikachu and a blaring Gameboy. Now picture an 83 year-old slightly bent woman in a mink hat carrying a shiny black purse and a hardback book. They greet one another in our living room, cautiously attempting to figure out what's behind the gear.

Grandma smiles and asks who the furry creature is under her granddaughter's arm. Abby introduces Pikachu. Grandma greets the long-eared monster with a thunderbolt tail warmly, and then her grandchild spouts Pokémon facts and features that would confuse any but another master. Soon they decide Grandma should read a book about

Pokémon to help her learn. My daughter picks *Pikachu's Vacation*. Its literary quality is well below zero.

The next day Abby creates a multiple choice test to check her grandmother's understanding. Grandma gets both questions right.

Gameboy sound-effects travel through the house. My child keeps that hand-held device with her constantly. When she tries to point out various Pokémon on the tiny screen, Grandma squints and nods. Then turns back to her own pastime, a recent novel by David Guterson.

The family reading book we just started is the third of a series about three orphans who are hotly pursued by an evil uncle. My daughter loves it, so we read together often.

As I read it now, however, I wonder if its portrayal of adults as silly and stupid is offensive to Grandma, who's sitting nearby quietly continuing her novel.

My son Justin arrives home from college toting a PlayStation 2. He waited in line all night at Wal-Mart to buy this just-released video game machine. After dinner, he and Abby settle in for a spell with the one game he has that she might like: Orphen, Scion of Sorcery.

The rest of us stand around to watch as my son fires up this highly appraised console and teaches his little sister how to play. It turns out Orphen's main task is to destroy multiple monsters that attack often. Grandma leaves the room after a few dozen blasts and one or two four-letter words. I'm not happy either, but a lot more tolerant of this junk that I was when my older two were young explorers of the same tasteless media.

Orphen is Teen-rated, I notice, while hunting through Justin's game collection for something more appropriate.

Generation Gaps and Bridges

Then I remember receiving a PlayStation game for review, The Wild Thornberry's Animal Adventures. I find it, and hand over the Everyone-rated game, and within minutes my 7 and 20 year-old kids are engrossed in the electronic fun. After that I join the non-techies in the other room.

Screen time is limited in our family, though when grown-ups come to visit, rules relax a bit so adults can chat while the youngest is otherwise occupied. That means more Gameboy, computer, and TV time. Playing kids' games, even electronic ones, I think, is more worthy than watching Nickelodeon, so I tend to allow extended play rather than another TV show.

Earlier that evening, Justin and his grandmother had a chat about Italy—his favorite European country (after visiting a few on a student trip last summer), and one of hers too. They joked about going there together some day. She'll take him to museums and talk about Italian Renaissance art. He'll take her to more hip haunts and demonstrate the art of people watching. Two different generations stretch each other to make a comfortable fit. I hope they do find a way to go some time.

On a previous visit, my mom-in-law had asked me for a computer tutorial. She had recently bought an iMac to write environmental reports and to email colleagues and relatives. Since then, she's managed with help from me and from her other grandkids when they come to visit her in New York.

It must be incredibly frustrating for her and other intelligent adults to struggle with technology while watching children learn as naturally as they learned to walk and talk. I think kids pick up the skills easily because computers and

Parenting Forever

other electronic toys are part of their culture, just like parlor games and French lessons were part of Grandma's.

When the Thanksgiving holiday is over and we're about to part, I think about three generations and how difficult or easy it can be to connect them. Grandma says when she was young, generations blended quite naturally because they were together often. Three-thousand miles separates us and visits are infrequent. "We have to depend on the phone and email," she says sadly.

Next time Grandma comes to visit she promises her youngest grandchild that she'll read another Pokémon book. Next time, I hope my youngest will choose to share her artwork and poems, instead.

Mike and I are now grandparents to four kids who range in age from 13 to 3 months. They all live nearby, so frequent interaction is easy. Mike and I have gotten to know the oldest, Landyn, as he and Justin lived with us for a while, and Landyn stays overnight occasionally, plus, we try to get to his baseball games and track meets. Even better, Landyn and Mike have designed and built several inventions together, including an airplane and bird house, among other creations.

The other three grandkids are all under five, so we don't know them as well, yet. However, all together we play games that range from trivia, ring toss, and various card games inside during the winter, to softball, Frisbee, beanball toss, and croquet outside when it's warmer.

True Confessions of Computer Love & Logic

It happened about a year ago, when I was fixing my son's computer. I sat up, took a deep breath, and released the truth. I love technology. I've buried it below consciousness for years, while claiming my attachment to the box-with-keyboard is purely professional. It helps me write better, I say, and keeps me in touch. Those advantages are true, but it's much more than that.

Never mind that I worked for Apple Computer when we lived in California, and wrote gigabytes of words about educational technology. Still, I wasn't a techie. No, it's what computers can do for us that's awesome, not what they are—plastic boxes that talk like Darth Vader or Poo-Chi, cost too much, and need fixing too often.

Anyway, we humanists (e.g., liberal arts majors) disdain computers because they're numerical and we're alphabetical. And because it's kind of a tradition to hate machines. Of course, humanists use computers for work; everybody does these days, but we don't praise them or play with them in public.

Still, I must admit to writing two books about technology in education. It was important to record what I'd discovered about teaching and learning with computers after working in schools for a dozen years.

A few birthdays ago, I asked my husband to give me a cell phone as a gift. It's critical to have a phone with me if the car breaks down, I told him. Well, it is.

Not long after that I bought a fax machine. It'll be useful, I rationalized to my husband. I set it up. I got us a second phone line for the fax and the computers. And the fax was useful until it was more hassle than useful, so we resumed going out to fax, but mostly we sent and received documents via email, which was a pretty good substitute most of the time.

Then I bought a scanner. It will enable us to send pictures, I told my husband. He chuckled. I installed it and digitized favorite family pictures. That brought me back to an old love, photography, which I had abandoned along with my dark room when our first child arrived.

Can you guess? Next it was a digital camera. That time the whole family got into the technology, meaning the kids took pictures and asked me to make them web-ready to email to friends and future friends.

What next? A Website, of course, to share photos, artwork, articles, and other information with extended family and whomever. After that, a CD burner and later an MP3 player to make music really portable.

Over the winter break, my son Justin brought his computer home from college so Mom could fix it. He couldn't get the modem to work. "You're the kid," I told him. "You're supposed to know more than I do about computers."

I grumbled through the first hour as I tried a dozen ways to activate the modem, then suddenly realized I was having fun. Maybe I should have gotten my son involved, but he was doing the collegiate thing. Sleeping.

It was a moment of awakening for me. Bells tolled inside as the truth struck—technology's not only useful, it's fascinating. It does exactly what I tell it to do, if I tell it right. Sort of like Simon Says, only this Simon's much fussier than any human. The intriguing part is getting the language right so that Simple Simon will respond. That's a language problem we humanists have to love.

So it's okay, after all, to be attracted to this little lump of plastic that doesn't appreciate fine art or literature. It does appreciate logical language, or at least, what it (or its programmer) thinks is logical. Ha, ha, that's the puzzle; I've got to figure out just what it understands and what it doesn't. The consequence of losing is machine failure, which is enough incentive to win. And since the little lump would probably rather compute than lie idle or get kicked, I figure it too, wants me to succeed.

Maybe I should wake my son to teach him how to fix his own PC. He probably should learn, but what should I say? "Grab some juice and join the fun? C'mon down and play Simon Says with your computer?"

Parenting Forever

I go upstairs, gently push his door open, and try the cheerful approach.

He rolls over and buries his head.

Maybe later. Maybe never. I think most people these days like technology okay, as long as it works.

I like it because it does things that are extremely useful, and some other things that are, well, fun. Next, maybe I'll try a Web phone, or curl up (?) with an eBook.

Now, so many years later, and equipped with an iPod filled with audiobooks, an iPad filled with e-books, a laptop for watching movies, a printer-with-scanner for scanning images, and a desktop Mac for writing books, searching the Internet, processing photos, and everything else, I'm still having fun. These lumps of plastic are constantly getting more capable and easier to use, so I'm still hanging on for the ride.

A Little Lapse of Manners

Suddenly my 7 year-old has become rude.

Or maybe, gulp, I've just started noticing. A few days ago, for example . . .

"You said draw!" she retorted when I read the spelling word *drawer* with a sentence, and she wrote *draw*.

"I'm sorry, but I said *drawer*—open the *drawer*," I answered calmly.

"No you didn't!" she snapped.

"Well, write *drawer* this time," I answered to avoid a scene. That was my first mistake, or maybe the zillionth.

When it was time for school, I held up her coat. "It's time to go, Sweetie."

She reached for her stuffed companion, but it wasn't there. "Where's Pikachu?"

"I don't know," I said, "but we have to go."

"I can't leave without Pikachu!"

Her three-second search failed to reveal the yellow monster.

"Why aren't you looking?" she scolded.

Then it hit me. My little one has promoted herself to Boss, and in the name of peace, I've let it happen.

Truth be told, my husband and I have been watching the bossiness build, but assuming—hoping?—it was within the range of acceptable. After all, our darling is sick, she's upset, she feels ignored, she . . until excuses run out and she's exposed as just plain rude.

No, actually, we're exposed as just plain dumb for not reading the signs and halting her ascension. Now our daughter has the power to challenge parental authority.

No child wants to be that powerful, but most children will try. My husband and I have been too busy or too amiable to stop the push for power.

This afternoon while collecting my daughter from school and allowing her sharp voice to roll off my back, I overheard another mother say to her child, "You better not ever speak to me like that."

Okay, I get it. Yes, I really do get it.

We will focus on the problem and deal with it. Now.

Plan of action: develop a handy set of logical consequences to issue whenever this child crosses behavior boundaries.

There will be one warning. Then, no dessert, no TV, or no Gameboy. Maybe extra chores, time out, or a written apology. Besides negative consequences, there will be rewards for improvement like a special outing, her favorite meal, a funny thank-you card or other treat.

The struggle to regain parental authority and decent manners has begun.

In the evening, while we're re-reading the second Harry Potter book, I think I remember the monster inside the chamber is a giant spider. Instantly my daughter's shrill voice, "No, it's not a spider."

This time I'm ready. "That was rude," I say calmly and firmly. "Can you think of another way to say what you think without being rude?"

"But it's NOT a spider!"

"You may be right, but you can't talk to people that way. Try, 'I don't think it's a spider, Mummy' in a polite voice.'"

"But it's NOT a spider!"

She stands resolute.

Finally, I say as calmly as possible. "You will have to find a nicer way to say that if you want the privilege of desserts this week."

She exits with clenched fists.

No progress this round, but it set a foundation of expectations. She's as stubborn as I am, and I'm not sure she fully understands the difference between saying what she thinks, and saying what she thinks, politely. Wish me luck.

By the way, the monster in the chamber is NOT a spider.

But she still has to be polite.

Now, I'm happy to report that Abby's very polite.

A Mother's New Groove

It must be a particular form of middle-aged madness. Suddenly, I have this overwhelming urge to break the routine and do something different—learn a new skill, renew an ancient one. Something active, like skating, diving, or dancing.

It's not a wish to abandon my job or may family, but to enrich us. After all, I can skate with my daughter, dance with my husband, swim and dive with everybody. I decide to try all of these and then pick one or two to continue.

First roller skating. I take my youngest, Abby, to the Roll-A-Way in Lynnwood—first time for her, first time in about 25 years for me. She clutches my hand, and my legs wobble mightily. But oh, it looks so beautiful when the experts do it, and after a while it feels a little like flying.

For days I fantasize about skating. Abby and I will get our own skates and practice doubles routines in the park. We'll be fantastic, and it'll be so special to have this shared interest.

To get our own skates, however, costs $60-$150 per pair, new. Worse, my daydreams are ambushed by touches of reality, like tripping on gum wrappers and breaking my brittle bones.

Never mind. I locate two pairs of roller skates for less than $50 total on e-Bay, the great Internet garage sale. As for breaking bones, maybe I'll wear pillows or make a pair of sweatpants out of foam rubber. Okay, well, that was an intriguing fantasy . . . Abby wasn't so keen on it anyway . .

So . . . how about swimming, and especially diving off a flexible board. I used to teach Red Cross Swimming classes some 30 years ago, but since then I haven't swum much, and almost never stepped out on a spring board.

So the three of us willingly go to the Mountlake Terrace pool on Sunday and we all plunge in. It's great to swim again, and I actually remember all the strokes. Then, I gaze up at the diving board and read the sign: Board Closed.

Oh well, even when it's open, I may not venture out there to embarrass my child with a mother's unpracticed dive, more like a belly flop. Besides, my daydream has me practicing in the dead of night until I can keep my legs straight and touch my toes for a perfect jackknife. Daydreams are definitely essential for happiness.

Another daydream I enjoy features me on the dance floor, graceful and adept. Not ballet or jazz or aerobic, but ballroom dancing, as in waltz, tango, swing, and cha cha. Yes, I can do this kind of dancing without looking like a middle-

A Mother's New Groove

aged idiot, and I can enjoy it with my husband, now and through age 60, 70, and beyond.

We're a little rusty, though. It's been years since the last dance we went to at Menlo College when I was teaching there. I go to the Internet and search on the keywords: ballroom dancing online instruction, and come up with diagrams of dance steps for the foxtrot and others.

Now for a place to actually dance. I search and find the Washington Dance Club in Seattle. Before their Friday night dances, they offer an hour of basics for beginners and folks like us who "used to" know the steps. If we decide to get more serious, we can take lessons locally at Jay & Lynn's Dance Workshop in Shoreline, or sign up for a class listed in any of the surrounding towns' recreation catalogs.

We decide to go dancing on Friday and catch the preliminary review. During the week I try a few steps while cooking dinner and pondering what to wear. I picture us waltzing around the floor looking oh-so-elegant, and then switching to an East Coast Swing that will cast off years and energize our souls.

The night before our big date, the babysitter cancels. Reality strikes again. So, we turn on the stereo and dance by ourselves, though there isn't a CD in the house with a foxtrot, waltz, or cha cha on it.

Now, you may hate the very thought of roller-skating, diving, or dancing, but surely there is *something* you would like to try? Singing, Calligraphy, Sailing, Yoga? Don't you ever daydream about picking up a new interest or revisiting an old favorite that's been buried over time by work and family?

Parenting Forever

Spring is a great time for starting something new. Besides, you can get your spouse or kids involved too. So no excuses. Pick something, and get out there and try it!

Now, in retirement, I made jewelry for a while, and loved creating enamel pieces, but then discovered that enamel powder is ground-up glass and I was breathing it, so I stopped. Mike is taking an assortment of classes, creating political cartoons, and teaching a class that analyzes political cartoons. There really is time now to learn new things, and we love it.

The Great Pokémon Turn-Off

Parenting challenges abound, it seems, and this is one I never faced with the two older children. My nearly 8 year-old has become obsessed with the Pokémon game in her Gameboy.

At first, my husband Mike and I were pleased to see Abby learning new vocabulary words from the screen displays and the guide book. We were encouraged by the complexities of the Pokémon's evolving characteristics, and the task of learning different strategies to overcome opponents. Plus, our daughter was motivated to use math skills that she usually hates to practice. So we let her play. And play. And play.

Parenting Forever

Now we're noticing other outcomes of this immersion. Our child wants to play every free moment of the day, and night. She carries her Gameboy everywhere. Attachment and loyalty are wonderful traits. But . . .

During the time at school, Abby talks with others who are equally enthralled. They imitate Pokémon characters during recess, share game strategies, and compare progress. Her enthusiasm, concentration, and motivation to learn are outstanding when the subject is Pokémon. Such thirst for learning is a parent's dream. But . . .

She is interested in nothing else. She craves more and more Pokémon. Her teachers report that she has trouble following directions and focusing on work, and she races through it with little concern for accuracy or quality.

This is a young video game player possessed by the game, I fear, and according to MIT sociologist, Sherry Turkle, when people play video games they do more than identify with a character on the screen, they act for it. For many, the goal isn't just a better score but an altered state.

Other child development experts claim that excessive viewing can affect children's attention and thinking abilities, their creativity, and their emotional and social development.

Education psychologist Jane Healy takes it further. A developing brain that encounters countless hours of TV or video games will be different from one that has not, she says. Intensive viewing can reduce stimulation to the part of the brain that's critical for development of language, reading, and analytical thinking. It can also discourage development of brain systems that regulate attention, organization, and motivation.

The Great Pokémon Turn-off

Besides these potential problems, there's the whole issue of media violence. Pokémon video games involve brutal combat between creatures—not humans, defenders are quick to point out—but violence just the same.

There's tons of research to show that watching screen violence can in fact cause more aggressive behavior in those who watch a lot of it. And, it doesn't take too many hours of watching Pokémon, Digimon, Dragon Ball Z, Duck Tales, and Tom & Jerry, to witness considerable violence.

My daughter is not violent. But I have noticed more irritability and rude behavior, such that recently I had to re-teach and re-enforce good manners.

Another concern arises as I watch young eyes staring at the tiny Gameboy screen. An hour or two a day of that kind of eye exertion can't be great for anyone's vision.

Abby no longer invents new characters and stories in her mind. Instead, imaginative play consists of role-playing various Pokémon, recalling their particular powers, and imitating the game as packaged.

Enough! It's way past time for the great Pokémon turn-off. My player has the vocabulary and the strategies, so all that's left is to "catch'em all," and there are over 200 of them. We'll pull out the batteries this Saturday.

My dearest is destitute. She thinks we hate her, because otherwise, why would we take away what she loves so much. I hold her in my arms and tell her that's how much we love her. But, of course, she doesn't understand.

On Saturday when the Gameboy is quiet, we play chess and tic tac toe, read stories, draw, skate, and other rediscovered joys.

Two weeks have passed and Abby is now inventing games as she used to. She's the family Crazy Eights champion, and she reads books again instead of screens.

I don't condemn Gameboy or Pokémon. My daughter learned a lot about how to travel in virtual worlds, how to strategize, and to feel competent with electronic devices. The problem arose only when the game became dominant, and that occurred so subtly that by the time I realized, it was too late.

When the Gameboy gets its batteries back in a month or two, I'll help Abby learn to balance all of her activities, rather than trade everything for a virtual life with Pokémon.

❊

Now, years later, Abby seems to have struck a better balance among her different interests and activities. Though she does tell us that her generation still loves Pokémon. The latest obsession is Pokémon Go, which sends kids outside to find Pokémon characters with their cellphones. At age 23, Abby's been spotted playing it with friends (some even older), as well as her karate students at the dojo.

Too Much Emphasis on Testing?

You be the judge.

Some states have imposed high-stakes testing programs for K-12 education. They're called "high stakes" because the state's student achievement exam is a significant determinant of students' placement, teachers' salaries and jobs, and continuation or termination of schools.

Look at Texas, for example. President Bush claims that Texas' students have made huge improvements as a result of high-stakes testing. Indeed students' scores on the Texas exam did rise significantly, and now Bush argues that his home state provides a model for how all students can excel.

A closer look at what really goes on in Texas, however, raises questions about the value of such high-stakes testing. A study completed last year by the Rand Corporation examines the gains in Texas and suggests negative consequences of high-pressure accountability systems.

One major negative is related to excessive teaching to the test. Students in Texas are being pushed to focus on the skills that are covered on the exam, at the expense of other important skills and subjects. Even the teachers report they're spending a lot of time preparing students for the test, and a lot less time on the rest of the curriculum.

Another negative outcome of high-stakes testing is cheating. An increase in cheating and other inappropriate activities has been documented in Texas and other states with high-stakes testing. It turns out that when people believe an imposed system is fundamentally unfair, and when their jobs depend on their students' test scores, it's not just the children who are motivated to take extreme measures to boost their scores.

Speaking of unfair, to this observer, it seems absurd to make teachers and schools solely responsible for a student's academic success, as if parental support, adequate food, enough sleep, and a decent place to study don't impact their learning.

Comparing state and national assessments, when Texas students' scores on the state tests are compared to their scores on the National Assessment of Educational Progress (NAEP), a whole different picture emerges. The NAEP exams are based on a national consensus of experts concerning what students should know and be able to do. They are generally recognized as the "gold standard" for comparisons.

On the NAEP tests, Texas' scores improved at about the same level as the national scores, even though they made much greater gains on the Texas state exam. Why the difference? The Texas exams are directly aligned to the state curriculum and are administered by the classroom teacher.

So what, you might ask? Why aren't huge gains in state exams enough to claim success? As the research points out, the intense pressure to raise students' scores on those tests has caused a narrowing of the curriculum as well as more unethical practices. Further, the Texas exam is said to focus on a more basic set of skills than the National exam.

Regarding the gap between White students and students of color, the state exams show a significantly diminishing difference, whereas the national exams show the gap in Texas is large and getting larger.

The Rand study doesn't suggest that states abolish state-level testing. However, it does suggest that to avoid the negative outcomes of high-stakes testing, states should use more criteria than just those tests to measure the success of students, teachers, and schools.

In Connecticut, for instance, the state disallows schools from using the state test scores to make decisions about students, teachers, and schools. Interestingly, Connecticut shows the largest gains in NAEP scores, and a decreasing gap between majority and minority students.

Other measures that can be used to assess students' academic success include: teacher assessments, portfolios of student work, and course grades. Measures of teachers' success can include: peer evaluations, subject-knowledge assessments, and video-examples of teaching. Fair assessment of schools might include: dropout rates, parent assessments, and outside experts' evaluations.

In our state, the Washington Assessment of Student Learning (WASL) exams have not yet been elevated to the high-stakes level of use as the sole measure of success for students, teachers, and schools. However, in 2008, the plan is to make passing of the 10th grade WASL mandatory for graduation.

The state's Academic-Achievement and Accountability (A-plus) Commission has been studying what consequences may be appropriate for educators and schools whose students don't pass the WASL.

Let's hope they consider research results concerning Texas and other states with high-stakes testing programs. Let them compare those systems with more promising examples of success such as Connecticut's. And let them not be tempted to rely on one test to judge the success of our state's students, educators, and schools.

Since I wrote this column, the nation has over-dosed on high-stakes accountability, through the No Child Left Behind law. Experience with this law and its consequences appear to have convinced policymakers and the public of the limitations of high-stakes testing. Now, a new federal law with less emphasis on testing is finally in place. Maybe we can refocus on teaching and learning again.

Back on a Mac

Whenever I write something that hints at comparison between Apples and Windows PCs, Macintosh users instantly are in my e-mailbox ranting about those "WinBoxes" they insist are incapable of functioning reliably. Of course, they claim Macs are flawless in function and form.

I was one of those Apple addicts even before the Macintosh was introduced (which happened while I was living in CA and working at Apple), until I discovered there were almost no Mac-compatible digital cameras, and CD burning required a clunky peripheral and lots of luck.

My switch to a Windows PC, happened after I started writing this *Seattle Times* column and discovered that most of you, dear readers, use PCs. I wanted to share your experience.

Parenting Forever

To my surprise, the Dell that started my PC experience worked quite well. Frozen screens occurred no more often than on my Mac. And I liked being able to use new applications and peripherals that hadn't yet been developed for Macintosh.

Recently, however, I've grown more worried about computer viruses and intruders, and the attack data add up to one huge difference between these systems. PCs are far more vulnerable to attack, because most malicious code is written for Windows, which is not as resistant, according to more than one technical expert, and so many more people have PCs that the attackers have more victims.

In addition, the past few years of innovations and zealous determination have totally transformed the Mac since I put mine in the closet. Maybe it's time to try Macintosh again.

So, with a new iMac on my desk, I get started with high expectations. The installation is easy. Photos look gorgeous. The colors look right and resolution is high.

I install AirPort to experience the joy of wireless networking in my home office. Indeed, installation is easy for people networking with just AirPort, but I'm installing it on top of an existing wired network, and Apple's directions for that are contradictory. I end up with a trial-and-error approach that finally works.

The well-reviewed iLife applications—iPhoto, iTunes, iMovie, and iDVD—at first seem overrated, especially after trying iPhoto's Enhance button and watching it ruin my pictures. I install my favorite slideshow-creation program, written for older Macs, and the screen freezes repeatedly, so I give up on that.

Back on a Mac

A couple of days into this and I haven't fallen in love yet. I'm no technology wizard, but Macs are supposed to be designed for folks like me.

I continue the experiment, but rather than try to make my old favorites work on the new Mac, I decide to adopt what's native to this machine and to look beyond the casual user's level to the core that is not just an operating system but a set of values.

I buy a couple of books because I learn better when a system is explained sequentially and the reference remains handy on my desk.

Then I sign up for an Apple Mail account. I move my whole photo collection to iPhoto and my music to iTunes and start looking closely at what's beneath each icon. I study the preferences for each application and tool, read about each, and try things.

I learn how to create an iPhoto slideshow and burn it on a CD, then burn several slideshows on a DVD with a menu that will play on my TV with a connected DVD player. The slideshows look good.

Using iTunes, I make up a playlist of classical music stored on my Mac and when friends come over, play it as background music. It sounds better than Beethoven on my stereo.

PDF (portable document format) is the Mac's default format for sharing documents, so Mac users can convert any file to PDF and send it to PC users who can open it with all the Mac fonts and formatting intact.

The more I explore this new iMac, the more I find. And now that I've tried both Mac and PC computers, it will be interesting to watch how they each evolve over time.

Parenting Forever

❋

This is one of the "Getting Started" columns I wrote for *The Seattle Times* from 2000 to 2007. Because I was a columnist who often used and reviewed new technology products, technology companies were happy to lend or give me their newest hardware, software, cameras, music players and other products. My kids were delighted to discover what new products arrived, and eager to play with Mom's latest techie toys.

Not long after I wrote this column, I was again fully attached to Apple computers, and the devices that came afterwards, including the iPod, iPad, iPhone, and various laptop computers as well. Back home again.

What to Do with a Reluctant Swimmer

At the age of one, my youngest happily played with me in swimming pools. At two, however, she accidently fell into a swimming pool during a family vacation, and since then she's hated those splashing, choking watery demons. After many efforts to entice her in again, she still wouldn't go near water, even at 3 and 4, and on up until 7, and then I really began to worry.

All her friends could swim, and when their birthday parties became swimming parties, Abby refused to go. I didn't force her to learn, figuring she would eventually choose to herself. But she didn't.

I worried about her being left out, but mostly about her safety. Living in this watery boat-loving area, it seems critical to be able to swim. I picture my daughter as a teenager going in a canoe with some friends and fooling around like I did as a kid. The boat tips over—it's part of the fun—and nobody had bothered to ask if everyone can swim.

Abby HAS to learn. The longer I wait to insist, the harder it will become for her later.

At five, I put her in a swimming class, and that torture lasted one lesson. I tried private lessons, but the sweet young teacher couldn't help my child overcome her angst.

After that I let it go for a while, silently searching for the right person—someone who would push Abby to face her fear and conquer it. Someone who could win my child's trust, and keep it.

Finally, I discovered Linda Riggins' swim school. Her pool is in Kirkland, a 40-minute drive from my home. Her classes are half an hour, four students per class, $20 a class, twice a week (recommended). She uses a flotation system, progressing from a few floats on the swimmer's back, to two, one, and then none. She's reputed to be particularly good with reluctant swimmers.

To me, the prospect seemed extremely time-consuming, expensive, and absolutely necessary. I signed us up.

My daughter entered her first class broadcasting that she hated swimming. She was the oldest by a few years, wore three floats on her back, and wouldn't put her face in at the beginning of the lesson.

By the end, she was on two floats, had dipped her head, and jumped off the side of the pool. Linda did not permit crying, would not accept refusal, and never pushed beyond the safe and the possible. My child adored her.

That was three months ago. Today, my swimmer races across the pool with no floats, and dives off the board. Still resistant to give up her identity as the one-who-hates swimming, she now says she loves "pooling."

We typically arrive at her lesson a little early to watch the class before ours. Abby enjoys watching the other kids. I enjoy watching their teacher. She teaches kids to swim, and she teaches me how to parent.

Once I watched her with a 5 year-old who had been taking lessons for many months, and was still wearing a half a float. At this lesson, Linda didn't put on the float, he panicked, and started crying loudly. She said he had to stop crying and talk to her. He didn't. She said if he kept crying his mother would have to leave the pool area. The boy finally stopped crying and said he needed his float. Linda put it on.

He crossed the pool a couple of times. Linda quietly removed the half float. This time she told him she would tuck it inside his suit. He was very unhappy, but swam, and did just fine. He crossed a couple more times with the float tucked in his suit.

When it was time to jump off the diving board, Linda held the float and he jumped. Then he swam without it. During play time at the end, the boy swam all around with no float, smiling broadly.

I've seen Linda deal firmly with a number of hysterical children who end up calm, happy, and extremely proud of themselves. At 59, this teacher applies a kind of tough love that is rare these days, especially the kind that also proffers humor and affection.

I'm not suggesting parents should adopt Linda's style of teaching at home. Sometimes I think it's our job to sooth our children's woes.

What I'm suggesting is that there is a time and place to be firm, and to push kids to do more than they think they can. I cherish those teachers who insist that children behave and perform at their best. I've seen it demonstrated over and over that adults who are tough and loving while pushing kids to succeed, will succeed.

I have strived for a similar balance of firmness and support in parenting, with varying degrees of success. Sometimes we need mentors, and personal help from others along the road to raising our kids to be competent and responsible adults. We parents welcome all the good help we can get.

Waiting to Fly, Again

It took over 24 hours, when it should have been six, for our family to fly to New Hampshire this summer. Last year was just as bad. Delays, cancelled flights, missed connections, and enforced layovers have become the norm for air travel, and it makes me furious.

Now, even the flight attendants are complaining about the airlines. They note that incidents of anger and abuse are increasing, and when fed-up passengers are on board, it's the flight attendants who have to deal with them. I sympathize with their plight, and their plea for more training to handle the 3,000-4,000 yearly incidents as well as better support for their efforts. But I'm one of the angry passengers. Politely fuming. Yes, I'm very polite, but I want more reliable, on-time flights so passengers won't be so angry and, incidents won't occur so often. And, so I'll get where I'm going on time.

Generally, I'm fairly patient with people, computers, and other naturally flawed systems. But I seethe when the excessively expensive systems provide very poor service. Especially when they could make small improvements, such as adding more leg room by dropping a few rows of seats and spreading out the rest.

No such luck. The spaces are shrinking and we're packed like pretzels.

On this trip, our flight was delayed leaving Seattle. We finally arrived in Chicago around 3 p.m., too late to catch the connection to Manchester or any airline flight to New Hampshire that day. Nothing flying to Maine, Vermont, or Massachusetts, either—we would have rented a car and driven the rest of the way from those places.

Instead, we had to wait for an 8 a.m. flight the next morning. Even that took us to Maine before turning around and dropping us in New Hampshire. We finally arrived at my Dad's house that afternoon, a whole day late.

Positive points of the tardy flight? My child didn't get airsick this time; I'd packed plenty of snacks in my carry-on bag; and the chief flight attendant made us laugh. She slipped little jokes into the totally tedious pre-flight and arrival announcements. As we taxied to the gate, everyone gave her a standing, er, seated-and-still-buckled ovation.

Our family didn't have to fly again for a week, so the frustration faded in our minds as the vacation passed. But the dreaded return trip arrived anyway, and much to our surprise, flying home was easy. No major delays and no canceled flights.

This time, we were lucky. Flight delays averaging over 50 minutes have increased by 58 percent and canceled flights by 68 percent from 1995 to 1999, according to the Transportation Department. In the last couple of years, the

Waiting to Fly, Again

problem has grown worse, complaints have escalated, and expectations for the future are dismal.

I can't change the airlines (but perhaps we all can if we put more pressure on them). Meanwhile, maybe I can help you endure the waiting/flying experience a little more easily. For those of you planning to fly with family this summer, here are a few hints that may help:

- Take direct flights to your destination whenever possible, because catching connecting flights is the biggest problem.
- Fly early in the day, so if you miss a connection it's more likely there'll be another flight later the same day.
- Pack overnight basics in your carry-on plus a variety of snack foods, a good book, and other things to do that can help pass the hours.
- Assume you'll have to manage a very long delay, and be prepared psychologically. Then, if all goes well, count yourself lucky.

This is clear vision looking back to my family's flying experiences over the past few years. If I had followed my own advice before now, I might have moaned less and relaxed more.

Good luck.

I wish I could say that flying has gotten better between then and now, but no luck. Most food from home that's in your carry-on is disallowed now and tossed out when you go through the very long security lines—which are a new delay added to the trip since terrorists decided to fly among us. Fewer flights are canceled because fewer flights are offered, with more seats more tightly crammed. Not fun. I have almost decided never to fly again, except my entire extended family lives 3,000 miles back East.

How Important are Pets?

Kids turn to their pets when they need comfort, companionship, or a confidante.

At least that's what a study of 7 to 8 year-olds by British psychologists reported a while ago. The full report indicates that kids' first choice is actually mom, second is dad, and third is the family pet. But their point is that pets rate higher than siblings, other relatives, and friends.

Pets aren't quite that high up on the emotional chain in our family. As vital as our dachshund Willow and cat Toasty are to the family dynamic, they're not that high up as confidantes or comforters for my 8 year-old daughter Abby.

Maybe that's because family members are always around, she has schoolmates to talk to, and a best friend for solemn secrets. To satisfy my daughter's lingering need to hug something soft, there's that curly-haired stuffed terrier with the floppy ears who lives under Abby's arm. No great need for comfort from squirming furries.

When it's bedtime and the night monsters creep out of the closet or crawl from under somewhere, my daughter needs serious protection. She needs Willow—the loudest bark in the neighborhood—to sleep on her bed and see that she's safe. Willow will keep the evil serpents at bay and the giant sharks who swim outside her window waiting. Willow, even as he snoozes under the blanket, will stand guard through the night.

Aside from night duty, the family dog is the Sunday-in-the-park playmate. He chases tennis balls, plays soccer, and attracts kids from all corners to come and play.

After dinner, while we humans enjoy family reading on the couch, the dog and cat nestle in between bodies and radiate heat, plus hairs and animal aromas. Routinely Toasty hops off, and then up on the counter to check for left-overs and drink the rest of somebody's milk. Of course, Willow has to go there, too, to watch the action and wait for a morsel to fall.

Abby takes the family pets for granted—they're part of the family furniture like her toys and older siblings. If they are sick or missing, she's concerned. If no human friend is available to play, the dog will do. But my child doesn't seek the dog or cat for hugs and comfort when she's sick, alone, or upset. Besides mom and dad, her stuffed animals remain her most essential companions in sickness and in health.

Maybe that's because she can control her stuffed pets. Unlike the live ones who don't obey her or play by her rules, the plush ones always cooperate. Plus, her stuffed pets don't wiggle when picked up; they don't get distracted and dash away; and they don't mind if she accidentally steps on their tails.

Is this unusual? Other parents I've consulted note similar patterns. When a live pet is no longer new, it slowly becomes more like a sibling—the second-best playmate and rarely a confidante. And like a sibling, Abby would be distraught if something happened to Willow.

I puzzle about what role pets really do play in a family. I don't see their major role as confidante or comforter, as that study suggests. Still, they're significant. They must be because over half of all American families keep some kind of pet.

Besides providing nighttime protection for the youngest in our family, having pets teaches her how to care for living things that can't care for themselves, and how to be responsible. Plus, pets can be infinitely entertaining.

Our dog, for example, will play any ball game, anytime, and the cat can jump amazing heights. They snuggle and hug us, bark too loud, and nag for attention. They shed hairs and have accidents inside, lick and rub faces. Willow carries his ball around pleading for a playmate. Toasty brings in his own playthings—mice, lizards, snakes, and birds. Our pets are both annoying and adorable. They may not be the best comforters, but as companions, they're great.

FLASH: Abby just read this column and disagrees. She says Willow IS her best companion, comforter, and confidante. And guess what? The researchers who did that study asked kids, not parents. What do we know?

❖

Parenting Forever

We're happily pet-free in retirement (though Mike wouldn't mind having one). Justin's family has two dogs, and occasionally Abby brings her cat to stay during school vacations. We'll see what happens when Abby graduates from college and likely lives here for a while.

Getting Connected with a Wireless Phone

Are you among the 40 percent of Americans who use wireless phones? Or maybe you're one of the resisters who wonders why those people want to carry their phones around everywhere.

My first wireless phone was a birthday gift from my husband in the early 1990s. I asked for it because I wanted to have a phone handy in case the car broke down with my own and other children aboard.

When my husband got his a year later, we started using them to coordinate transportation for our kids. We also used them to confer while shopping, and to call home if we were going to be late.

Parenting Forever

We're the kind of mobile phone users who rarely leave our phones on, and seldom go over the limited minutes allotted on our shared service.

At home, my husband and I use the family "landline" phone to get information and to talk with family and friends. But we abhor the sales calls and campaign calls, and especially those that rudely ring during dinner and afterwards when we're relaxing. That's the downside of landline phones.

Years after we got our rather primitive cellphones, our older children got more modern cellphones, which fit right into their lifestyle. These easily portable personal communication devices enable them to keep in constant contact with friends as "Call me," may be the most common two words in their language.

Unfortunately, "Take me out to the ball game," and other questionably musical ring tones erupt from my son Justin's pocket and my daughter Molly's purse day and night while they're home on vacations.

Molly uses her cellphone to call college friends around the country because long distance is free. She uses her cell to look up movie times while out with friends. And she uses it to locate particular stores, followed by consulting MapQuest for directions to get there.

Justin also calls friends, makes plans to meet with other friends, or take a girlfriend out. Plus, he uses his cell to catch up on sports news, or check a few stores for items of interest. On the way home, he calls to ask what's for dinner.

When I need the kids for something, I dial their cellphone numbers. That's the positive side for parents. If our kids carry cellphones, we can reach them easily. Plus, with these in their pockets, my kids call home more often.

Connecting with a Wireless Phone

The down side for users is that carriers are still struggling to provide dependable service with fewer fades and disconnects. Voices deteriorate as I walk down the street, for instance, and calling from the local supermarket isn't possible. Still, most calls are clear, and uncertainty is "just the way it is," my kids say.

One thing I really like about my cell is that I can always turn it off.

If you're interested in going wireless, there are service plans to fit almost everyone's needs. Estimate how much you'll use the cell during the weekdays and weekends, pick a plan with enough minutes per month at a price you can afford. Make sure it includes free long distance from your calling plan area.

Some carriers provide wireless Internet access and email. If that's of interest, find out about the extra costs and capabilities as each provider is different.

Each provider also has its own unique features. Ask about them and decide if any are important enough to influence your choice. For more information on wireless phones and selecting a service, use the Internet to search for advice.

So much has changed since this column was written 16 years ago. Now, over 90 percent of Americans have cellphones, cellular service reaches all but the more remote areas (usually rural mountainous regions), and unfortunately, it's harder to find cellphone service that's inexpensive.

Parenting Forever

    Many of us consider owning a cellphone essential—to get help when we need it, locate ourselves and directions to where we're going, and for other personal essentials. Current cellphones have good-quality cameras and the ability to send the photos & video clips to others and/or post them on the Internet. Cellphones can also store and play back music and movies. These little hand-held, pocket-kept devices are considered essential by most of us, and many users don't even have home phones anymore.

    My kids can hardly remember or imagine a pre-cellphone world. Their cellphones go with them everywhere. Even old folks like me keep our cellphones handy, most of the time.

Thoughts on Living with Terrorism

Talk of terrorism and war dominates daily conversations around our dinner table. We share what we think about our country's vulnerability, how President Bush is doing, what the flag means, if God should be part of the national rhetoric . . .

Debates about whether we should drop bombs ceased with the first round in October. Now we discuss the need for collaboration and better intelligence to win this war. Along with these thoughts is the realization that we must improve America's image abroad.

But right now, our strongest, sometimes silent feelings come from fear. Yes. As much as we want to present a noble nobody-can-scare-us face to the world, the fact is, we're scared. We know that chemical, biological, even nuclear ingredients are in the hands of terrorists, and that terrifies us.

But, we're Americans. We're courageous, and we're dammed if we will let the enemy destroy our spirit and our way of life.

So we smile. We go to Saturday soccer games and the usual social gatherings. We laugh and we carry on at work and at home. We pretend life is like it was before September 11, 2001, and we know it isn't.

While we do all these normal things, we also wonder how America can end or even diminish terrorism.

You may have pushed our government to attack Afghanistan, while I lobbied to hold fire until soldiers can take aim at a clearly identified enemy. You may want to send more troops, while I want to gather more allies.

We may advocate different methods of fighting this war, yet we don't make the decisions even though we share the consequences of our government's actions.

We may feel powerless and vulnerable as individuals, while hoping our leaders will use their power wisely to keep America strong and us alive.

As we exercise our cherished right to disagree with each other and our government, remember that we are indeed in this together. When trouble hits, we will help each other. New Yorkers have shown us that. Those ordinarily feisty folks were comrades and heroes in their time of tragedy, and we will be, too, if it comes to that.

Maybe that's another place where fear seeps through our hearts and souls. What would we do on a hijacked plane, burning building, or small-pox infested city?

Barbara Kingsolver recently wrote on being a good citizen: September 11 is the worst thing that's happened, but only this year . . .

"Two years ago an earthquake in Turkey killed 17,000 in a day, babies and mothers and businessmen, and not one of them did a thing to cause it. Almost 60 years ago American planes bombed a plaza in Japan and more humans died at once than anyone thought possible. Seventy thousand in a minute. Imagine. Then twice that many more, slowly, from the inside," Kingsolver wrote.

There are a hundred ways to be a good citizen, Kingsolver suggests. "One of them is to look at the things we don't want to see. In a week of terrifying events, here is one awful true thing that hasn't much been mentioned: Some people (not just terrorists) believe our country needed to learn how to hurt in this new way."

She continues, "We have dropped bombs on others in the name of justice, but unlike most of the world, we have not suffered great losses on our own soil." (She omits here the Civil War that was fought on our own soil, with many, many lives lost.)

"The whole world grieves for us," Kingsolver writes. "And it also hopes we might understand from the taste of our own blood that no military weapon ever made can destroy hatred."

Personally, I hope that as we build new coalitions with other countries, we will also nurture long-term friendships rather than temporary alliances for a common cause.

Terrorists' hatred for America isn't totally without reason. Yet their acts are twisted and irrationally evil. They must be stopped. We, along with our allies, have to fight back, and we have to win this war to live safely again. At the same time, we also must begin a new era of improved relationships around the globe.

    I wish I could say that President Bush's wars in Afghanistan and Iraq did bring about peace in that part of the world, and managed to end terrorism. But, fighting in the Middle East has continued, increased, and ignited ISIS, which appears to be the greatest threat to Western countries as it's a terrorist war of incidents aimed against all who don't share their particular sect of ancient Islamic faith. We strive to manage fear, and we struggle with what it means to be a strong, tolerant, and fair American.

Finding that Holiday Feeling Again

The holidays have been slowly evolving at our house since the two older children started college. They still come home for Christmas, but are no longer here to help pick out and decorate the tree.

It's already up and lighted when they arrive, and eager to abandon ties with childhood, they remove those ornaments made in kindergarten, elementary, and even junior high.

Our Christmas morning begins later now, though the youngest manages to drag her older brother and sister out of bed hours earlier than their usual.

Stockings first. Breakfast, and then the great unwrapping. Abby, the 8 year-old, is delighted with each colorful box and its contents. Justin and Molly aren't quite so thrilled with all they receive. Indeed, in recent years, they've developed a new tradition that includes an after-Christmas shopping spree when they trade their parents' taste in clothes and music and accessories for their own.

I've given up worrying about whether they're being rude by not pretending to like what I've chosen. I'd rather they have what they really want. Besides, the 50 percent they do like is received with honest joy and thanks. Enough to keep me hooked on the game—the annual hunt for the perfect gifts.

Still, it's beginning to feel a little old. The morning of bottomless bounty no longer seems quite right, especially this year.

Instead of giving them what they probably won't like along with the sales slips, I plan to wrap up a few things from their explicit lists along with a Christmas check. Yes, we've come to that, and to avoid the void of few packages to open, there are some all-family gifts—a new XXX (I'd better not tell just in case they read this) we'll all enjoy on that day and beyond.

It's transition time, I suppose, when children become adults, and when piling on the gifts and watching their responses is no longer appropriate.

My older ones do appear to be growing with grace. I've noticed gentle humor in receiving those unwanted gifts, and now they care a lot more about giving.

Still, toning down Christmas is not easy. Not for this Mom anyway.

Some families do it by going away over the holiday. Friends of my daughters are flying to Hawaii, for instance. But with a young one, who still believes in Santa, we're not yet ready for that. We'll leave the day after Christmas, instead.

Finding That Holiday Feeling

Off to Florida to visit extended family, and that, at least, will help shift the focus from things to people.

Even so, giving my kids less is stressful for me, and as the shopping days before Christmas pass, I find myself retreating from the task and coming home with bags full.

Yes, of course, I could give those extra gifts to families in need, and in fact, we are helping a foster family celebrate the holiday. Still, it would be good for me to give less to my own and for them to expect and receive less. Fighting the spirit of Christmas greed is a noble cause.

Wish me luck. I'm trying to control the impulse to buy more, but my willpower is fading. Today's mantra: Less is more. More is less . . .

We did manage to come to a happy solution for giving gifts at Christmas . . . I pick out gifts for the grandkids (with advice from their parents) that they open on Christmas morning, and restrict buying for my adult kids and kids-in-law to a gift that's not too expensive, plus a check.

Learning to Type

When I was in fifth grade, my sister and I jointly received a Smith-Corona typewriter for Christmas. I was thrilled and, ignoring all other gifts, opened the booklet that came in the box and started teaching myself to type.

I studied the diagram that showed where fingers go on the keyboard and began typing—asdf jkl; adfs jl;k—while memorizing finger positions for the home keys. Then the extended keys, over and over, until I could type without looking at the keyboard.

My sister, who didn't care about 10-finger typing, managed to talk our mom into typing her school papers. But I had the better deal, I thought, because I kept control over my essays.

A generation later, my daughter Abby says she's learned to type at school, sort of, but mainly relies on the single-digit-approach.

Now's the time, I decide, to explore software typing tutors and pick one that can teach her finger positions, provide appropriate practice for each skill level, and motivate her to use the skills whenever she writes with a keyboard.

I try four popular typing tutor programs myself, and eliminate the first because I can't find an easy way for beginners to start by learning the home keys.

The next one is better. It includes beginner's lessons for any age level and a diagram of finger placement and practice exercises that are appropriate for each level. Intermediate typists can take a diagnostic typing test and enter at a higher level. But, its finger placement diagram isn't very clear, and its process of highlighting the key being typed is extremely distracting.

The next typing tutor program is better with a clear sequential teaching style, moving from one level to the next after passing a diagnostic test for that level.

The best tutorial, I think, is Type to Learn. Unfortunately, it's also the most expensive for home users because Sunburst focuses on school sets and doesn't offer a consumer version.

Type to Learn is designed for young learners through adults. Lessons begin with the home keys and learners fairly quickly move on to reaching for keys, with both hand anchored on the home row. The program waits for you to correct mistakes and notes accuracy at the end of each session. It also provides some practice games.

Now, there's still that tricky issue of carry-over. Do any of these electronic tutors motivate learners enough to use 10-finger typing whenever they write on a keyboard?

Frankly, I don't think any tutorial, by itself, can inspire learners to memorize keys and type with both hands unless the tutorial helps them reach mastery fairly quickly. Mastering the skills is the true motivator for continued use.

When people are comfortable using 10 fingers on the keyboard, they naturally type faster without having to look at the keys. At that point, their eyes are free to watch what they're writing on the screen or transcribing from a page. Successful learners feel empowered, and that's the motivation that's needed to keep using the skills.

Unfortunately, my daughter didn't become competent enough at school to use 10-finger typing regularly, so I devise a more personal curriculum that's more direct and works better. Since then, her competence is growing as she has more papers to write for school.

Abby is now an adult and can type better and faster than I can, and she's even earned money by transcribing recorded interviews done by UW grad students. My other two kids type pretty well too. Unfortunately, my husband still hasn't learned, though he does type pretty fast with two fingers, but with enough typos to cause him to vow to learn "some time." As a retiree, he now has the time, but some old dogs, you know. . .

The Ritalin Dilemma

Ritalin. Does the word conjure thoughts of an irresponsible drug-the-kids nation in which prescriptions for Ritalin have more than tripled in the last decade?

Or, does the mention of Ritalin evoke a sense of relief that children with attention-deficit-hyperactivity disorder (ADHD) are finally able to settle down and behave, and perhaps even concentrate a little better than the drug-free ones?

Several recent books—*Ritalin Nation*, *The Hyperactivity Hoax*, *Running on Ritalin*—argue that ADHD and Ritalin are the byproducts of our hyperactive culture loaded with intense video games, TV, rock music, and crammed schedules. Overstimulation runs rampant.

Children, by nature, have lots of energy. But today's kids are expected to stay seated and perform better at a younger age. They eat more high-calorie foods but get less exercise. No wonder they're hyperactive.

Some say that children in our culture do have an attention deficit—they get less attention from teachers who have more students to manage, less attention from parents who work more, and less time with other older relatives and caring adults.

I believe these arguments and flatly disdained Ritalin, until I read an in-depth article in *The New Yorker* (Feb. 15, 1999) which reported further information that hasn't been popularized.

The article acknowledges that all too often the criteria for prescribing Ritalin rest on casual responses such as: this child often has difficulty organizing tasks, doesn't seem to listen when spoken to directly, is easily distracted, and often acts as if driven by a motor. These "symptoms" describe children that many of us would consider normal.

However, there are other, more sophisticated evaluation procedures sometimes used that point to a different picture of ADHD. For example, when a child is asked to read as quickly as possible five rows of letters repeated in different orders, the ADHD child completes the task more slowly and often feels exhausted afterwards.

Another task involves estimating time passed. The ADHD child's estimates are way over, as if 10 seconds was much longer. ADHD kids often have trouble with punctuality and patience.

ADHD children tend to like video games that encourage fast, impulsive play, but are not as successful because they don't stop and think—even briefly—before reacting. In math, for instance, they may not be able to focus long enough to solve the problem, even though they may be smart enough.

An ADHD child is easily distractible and unable to self-regulate behavior—they're not always hyper or inattentive, but behavior varies from moment to moment.

The article reports that ADHD is 70 percent genetic. The other 30 percent may be from fetal environment, early illness, injury, or other causes. Experts are looking at neurology and the influence of specific genes rather than cultural and environmental causes.

Another way to understand the ADHD-Ritalin issue, according to the article, is to look at the body's use of dopamine. Dopamine is the chemical in the brain that affects attention and inhibition. When you focus on a complex problem, you generate a lot of dopamine. A person with ADHD has a lower level of dopamine. Ritalin raises that level.

Interestingly, Ritalin is not the only drug that enhances dopamine. Cocaine and Nicotine do too. Ritalin, however, does not cause lung cancer, it's not addictive, and its effect is more specific.

The article notes that untreated ADHD kids are much more likely to smoke and take illegal drugs in later life. The theory is that they're self-medicating with such drugs. Ritalin could be viewed as a safe alternative to more dangerous dopamine boosters.

Still, medicating children in huge numbers is upsetting, no matter what the explanation, and I'm not at all convinced the three million children believed to have ADHD need to take Ritalin.

Indeed, Ritalin is also becoming popular among teenagers and young adults. On campus, it's called the "cramming drug" because it keeps students awake to study and more focused during exams. One campus survey revealed that one in five of its students used the drug during finals.

Where is this kind of behavior headed? I read an article by a doctor suggesting that Ritalin should be more freely administered to children and adults who desire this sort of mental assistance. Think about it. Is that what we really want to do to ourselves?

Now, 14 years later, ADHD is not in the news very much these days, though the estimate reported in the National Health Interview Survey (NHIS) in 2013 is that about 9.5 percent of American children 4-17 years-old have been diagnosed with ADHD. Recommended treatments now advocate a combination of behavior modification and medication.

Heroes, Role Models, Mentors

When I was ten, Tenley Albright was my hero. She won an Olympic Gold Medal in figure skating and was studying to be a doctor. At the time, my own figure 8's were wobbly and my grades in science were not exactly pointing toward medical school.

Years later, when I had clearly aligned with the arts side of Arts & Sciences, my heroes still seemed superhuman, like novelist Barbara Kingsolver and syndicated columnist Ellen Goodman. However, by then, I'd adopted other more reachable kinds of heroes, as in role models and mentors, who seemed more real. Mentors, I think, are most important because they do what we aspire to do and help us learn how.

My first mentor was the teacher who supervised my internship when I was learning to teach English. I yearned to be as competent as she, and her guidance lit the way.

Then, after teaching for a dozen years, I chose another path, and another mentor who was a writer. In fact, each time I make a career change, I choose new role models and mentors.

Now, as a parent, I wonder about heroes and mentors and how they're viewed by young people today.

I read somewhere that people, especially adolescents, need heroes to learn about courage, noble purpose, and the art of reaching beyond oneself to achieve greatness. Adolescents also need role models and mentors who embody such qualities at human levels. I think we all do.

Actress Jodie Foster, who graduated from Yale University magna cum laude and has been a role model for aspiring actors, once said, "A real hero for me is a woman who has five kids and no money and takes care of them and survives."

Jane Seymour, who played Dr. Quinn in "The Heart Within," has said, "One of the most important things about Dr. Quinn is that she inspires young women to become doctors. She also inspires young boys to respect women."

There's a Website on the Internet, www.myhero.com, that invites readers to post stories about their real-life heroes. The site is a nonprofit educational project that aims to "remind us that we all have the potential to overcome great obstacles and achieve our dreams by following in the footsteps of our heroes."

Heroes, role models, mentors—the terms have become almost interchangeable these days, and I suppose it doesn't matter. What does matter, however, is that adolescents increasingly are adopting as their heroes athletes, actors, and musicians who behave badly and exhibit a lack of common decency.

Today's "heroes" are often wealthy, flamboyant, under 30, and though they may have considerable talent, they fail to live like heroes. Why are the rich and rude so appealing to some kids? These antiheroes say and do whatever they please, and believe themselves to be above rules and common courtesy. Yet, they're forgiven by fans, over and over, until young malleable minds believe those characters to be true role models.

Perhaps. And yet, I hope our youth know better, and that idolizing antiheroes is just part of their rebellion against authority, and a normal part of growing up.

Even so, it's our job to tactfully point out good & bad behavior, tolerance & intolerance, kindness & cruelty in everyday life as well as in the lives of their heroes and ours.

In my fifties, I'm once again scanning the horizon for heroes and role models to help guide me through the golden years. Newspaper columnist, Ellen Goodman, hovers closer to my grasp these days, while Barbara Kingsolver still floats in the stratosphere as my novels fail to obtain a publisher.

When we move closer to our life goals, perhaps earlier heroes transform into real people and wishful aspirations become possible. As I cycle back to youth for a moment, I wonder if, Dr. Tenley Albright, the Olympic gold medal-winning skater, is any more reachable now than she was then.

Me on skates again? Ha!

Parenting Forever

Now retired, I'm wondering about mentors and role models for folks like me, who have little desire to join groups or attend regular meetings. I look forward to finding some.

The Modern Little Red Schoolhouse

There are four children in my daughter Abby's third grade. In addition, two fourth graders, two second graders, and seven first graders share the classroom with two teachers. It's a little red schoolhouse in spirit, with a modern curriculum and highly competent teachers.

The school is Pacific Montessori Learning Center in southwest Edmonds, WA, and unlike some others, this one adapts the Montessori principle of individual hands-on learning to the current need for both solo and collaborative work to reach a higher level of achievement.

Whenever I walk into my daughter's classroom, there's a lot going on. In one corner, a teacher might be giving a math lesson. At other tables, children could be working together on projects or doing their own work. The other teacher would be helping students elsewhere in the classroom.

In such a small school, I can talk with either teacher about my child before or after school, and they both know how she's progressing as well as the details of her daily life at school.

Academically, I like the reading curriculum because it focuses on phonics, while accepting my child's natural preference for sight reading. The math curriculum includes Montessori materials in the pre-school, then shifts to the widely used Chicago math in first grade. It's a natural progression that also prepares kids for the move to another school (Pacific ends after 4th grade).

The two pre-school classrooms (for ages 3-6) each have around 20 children and two teachers, which works well as kids that age are learning how to manage themselves in group situations.

When my daughter was in the preschool, I was awed when first entering her classroom to see small people move around doing their work with so little commotion. Sometimes I'd shake my head imagining I was watching miniature adults in an office. Then one of them would slurp paint, another would giggle, and I knew this was preschool.

A hundred years ago, Maria Montessori developed specific learning materials and encouraged kids to interact with them in ways that would help them acquire a progression of skills and understandings. Her program demonstrated that children can enjoy mastering new skills and can concentrate for long periods in a stimulating environment.

Stimulating environment—if you've ever visited a Montessori preschool classroom, you may have left thinking the materials that sit neatly on low shelves around the classroom couldn't be more boring. A tower of pale pink blocks; stencils; colored pencils beside a pile of note paper; a tray with pitcher, cups, and tweezers.

But, watch the kids working with those materials and you'll notice they are happily focused on mastering a few specific skills, like pouring, cutting, adding and subtracting beads, identifying smells, writing letters, and reading words. Many children (but not all) are motivated to learn in this quietly stimulating environment.

Frankly, I'm delighted this school doesn't cater to the notion that fast and flashy is the way to capture kids' attention.

In some Montessori schools, teachers insist that children use the materials exactly as they were intended. Some schools provide only Montessori-designed materials. Others, like Pacific, apply the Montessori approach to new materials of their own invention. Pacific's teachers also believe in exploration, allowing children (within reasonable limits) to experiment with alternative ways to interact with the materials.

A special touch for this year in the elementary classroom has been the daily poetry reading which started with the teacher reading a short poem every morning, and has evolved into kids bringing poems, and some writing their own. They take numerous field trips (easier with such a small group); music and Japanese language teachers come twice a week, and after school there are Neo Art and Mad Science classes for those who choose to participate.

After six years of Pacific, my daughter's transition to public school next year will be major. She's reluctant to change, but with a good foundation from Pacific, she'll be fine.

Parenting Forever

❋

All three of our kids got their school start in Montessori schools, and we support their approach to learning. However, the culture and materials were not a perfect fit for all three. The Montessori schools that are flexible enough to adapt and even bring new materials into the curriculum to accommodate different children's needs are the best, in our opinion.

Home Course in Film History

My husband and I don't go out much. Our youngest keeps us pretty busy, so by Saturday night, our idea of fun is to curl up on the couch and watch a movie. We're a little fussy about quality, though, and it doesn't take many Saturdays to cover the year's best films.

So, we've started to dig into the past. It all began when we re-watched Lawrence of Arabia (1962), which motivated us to see more of director David Lean's work. Pretty soon we'd watched at least a half dozen of this films, including: Great Expectations (1947), Oliver Twist (1951), The Bridge on the River Kwai (1957), Dr. Zhivago (1965), and A Passage to India (1985).

It was fun to study a director's style by viewing his work, reading his biography, and discussing recurring themes over Sunday breakfasts and evenings after Abby had gone to bed.

When we'd seen all we could find of Lean's movies, Saturday night was dull until we discovered the American Film Institute's list of the 100 greatest American movies, here: http://www.filmsite.org/afi100filmsA.html.

It was time to create our own home course in film history by picking from the list and watching films in chronological order. We would also read reviews and sections from film history texts. The local video rental places don't carry many old movies, but our library does, and we can keep movies a whole week for free.

The first movie we watched was a classic: D.W. Griffith's silent film, Birth of a Nation (1915). We knew nothing about it. Our preconceived notion of early films was based on The Three Stooges and Charlie Chaplin movies, so we anticipated light humor with maybe a touch of social consciousness.

We were naïve beginners in film history.

During this over two-hours epic, Griffith attempted to cover U.S. history from pre-Civil War unrest through the war and post-war reconstruction. The first half of the movie presented predictable themes including close friends from the North and South finding themselves on opposite sides of the battlefield.

The second half covered the birth of the Ku Klux Klan (KKK) during the Reconstruction period. Here the film's contribution to social consciousness turned out to be a rather shocking portrayal of the KKK as the savior of White dignity and power in the South. It conveyed a deeply troubling message supporting White supremacy. During Civil War reconstruction this point of view wouldn't have been surprising, but the film was made 50 years later and its release prompted 20th century White supremacists to act.

Historically, the KKK waned after Reconstruction; however, when the movie was released in 1915 (it was one of the biggest box-office hits of all time) the KKK was effectively reborn. Today the KKK still uses this film for recruitment.

Perhaps the movie would have been dropped from film history if it hadn't included so many remarkable innovations. It pioneered night photography, for example, and the use of natural landscapes as background. It was the first to dramatize history in a story with authentic costuming, scenes with hundreds of extras, cross-cutting between scenes to create suspense, and building to a dramatic climax. It introduced new camera techniques such as using circular masks to open or close a scene, panning the camera to track movement, total-screen close-ups and fade-outs, panoramic and high-angle shots. Many are now standard techniques, but they were first used in this film (source: www.filmsite.org/birt.html).

Such a powerful movie—for its remarkable techniques and its appalling message. The taint of racism sent us back to film history books and further searches for information about D.W. Griffith. Not surprisingly, he was raised in the South, his father fought in the Confederate army, and D.W. was adamantly against any social mixing of races. Clearly, the film is an example of how art can reflect certain beliefs of the artist's time and place.

Our next movie, All Quiet on the Western Front (1930), dropped us into the trenches of WWI to experience war through the eyes and minds of several young German soldiers.

Undaunted, we march on, one Saturday to the next. Armchair history perhaps, but it prods our thinking and sends us back to books for more knowledge.

We made it through most of the American Film Institute's list, one rented DVD at a time. Our movie-watching habit has continued over the years, though now with vastly expanded access to movies and TV series through Netflix, Comcast On-Demand, and various streaming sources. We don't even have to drive to a Blockbuster video rental store anymore (besides the fact that they no longer exist). The large number and variety of choices does not always include old classics, however. We look forward to a future when all movies will be readily and easily available at home. For free would be nice, too.

Anxiety at Home a Growing Concern

There has been plenty of media coverage of anxious Americans these days. It's pretty clear that September 11, 2001 and its aftermath have made us more tense. Other cultural factors also contribute, including increased job insecurity, divorce rates, mobility, crime, and mistrust. Use of anti-depressants and tranquillizers is at an all-time high.

I, too, am one of the worriers. I worry about the world and about my kids. Recently, for example, I've spent way too much emotional energy worrying about the Middle-East, current domestic policies, my oldest child's relationship concerns, and my youngest child's transition to a new school.

Last week I read about a study that notes the rise in adult and child anxiety levels started well before September 11th.

Parenting Forever

Evidently, we began to worry more back in the 1950s, and now some say we're living in an Age of Anxiety.
The study reports that today's children are far more anxious than we were as kids. My youngest certainly is. I've tried to protect 9 year-old Abby from the scary images and talk of terrorism, but it's everywhere. Magazines and newspapers around the house display war and violence. People at the check-out counter discuss a possible attack on Iraq. Officials announce the latest terrorist alert on a TV blaring in the local Blockbuster video store.

Since last fall, Abby won't go upstairs by herself. She takes her dog into her bedroom at night for protection. Often she's afraid to sleep alone and pleads for me to stay with her. She thinks the neighborhood noises come from burglars, and if the dog barks, she's positive we're about to be assaulted.

When I share this with the mother of another 9 year-old, she tells me her child has nightmares almost every night. I talk to their teacher who says there are many in the class who are afraid.

So, is my daughter phobic, or is daily fear becoming a personality trait of this generation? Regardless, I want to help her. I call a therapist friend who advises me to talk with Abby about the anxiety and help her think of ways to comfort herself, sleep, and ease that fear of the unfamiliar. In essence, my role is to honor the fears and help her develop skills to cope with them.

The same night, before having the suggested parent-child conversation, there are frequent trips to our bedroom. Abby says she's too scared to sleep by herself. My husband Mike suggests she practice yawning. When that doesn't work, he rubs her back.

Anxiety at Home

A few minutes later she's back in our room, so I suggest she tell stories to Willow, and listen to quiet classical music. Then, finally, I tell her to count up to a thousand dogs, very, very slowly. Sometime after that she falls asleep by herself.

The next day, I talk to Abby about her fears and ask her to suggest ways that she can comfort herself. She says she doesn't know and that she can't help it. I suggest she read to Willow and rub his back so he can fall asleep. He needs more sleep, I tell her.

At night we go through the same routine. It's hard to be patient at midnight when Abby won't even try to calm herself. She just wants me to stay with her. I've done that before, but this time I tell her to bring a blanket and pillow into our bedroom and camp on the floor. No music, no light, no talking. That quickly becomes the pattern of our nights.

We talk about what might be causing so much angst. After all, she's been sleeping by herself for years. Besides a rise in anxiety since September 11, I know she's worried about starting 4th grade in a new school that's much bigger than the school she's been attending for the past six years. She affirms both fears, and others.

I'm thinking of taking her to a counselor, but doubtful it would help, and for now relying on a combination of two respected remedies; one is to build a resistance by exposing her to little doses of her fears, and the other is to reason through them so she can conclude they're not worth worrying about. Exercise and a healthy diet also help reduce anxiety.

Finally, for two nights in a row she manages to sleep by herself. That's progress. Learning to confront anxiety and comfort oneself is an important skill, and one that's not just for kids.

Parenting Forever

We made it through that episode and others. Now, both Abby and her parents need to continue confronting our fears as it is an anxious time for all of us across the country. In the current presidential campaign, for instance, one candidate is basing his campaign on fear, and advocates keeping out all refugees, Muslims, and other non-White, non-citizens. That's not who we are, and that's definitely not the America we want to be.

A Tale of Two Photos

Old flowers attract my attention today. A solitary fuchsia by the door wearing ragged petals and brown leaves. At the far wall, scarlet geraniums are bolstered by tiny buds about to bloom among dead and dying remains of summer.

With the flower season long past, I hadn't noticed these still living on the deck. Today, however, I was testing a new camera and looking for a subject. No other humans at home, so I hunted for something else alive to photograph.

There they were. Dots of color almost buried by fallen leaves and brittle branches. I walked closer and they grew larger—rich hues, standing firm, silent and unnoticed until now.

I stood in the cold wet wind studying those old things. Held a camera to my eye and searched for proud presence—

life past spring and summer, wiser now while yielding to bitter winter. I see it. Almost human in posture.

The elderly geranium bends forward, nods and whispers it has seen many things that I have not, yet. Not until I will stay and watch long enough.

The coral rose that my lens found by the garage is a picture now that speaks to me. There are age spots on its pale petals and tiny aphids along the stem I tried to rub away, but missed some that may hasten a natural death due soon.

This wise old rose talks to me of living and of aging. Of holding still and listening, of seeing new colors, forms, and motion. Of swaying with the wind and noticing how one can bend and still stay grounded. Of freezing and burning, bruising and tearing surfaces that test and strengthen one's resolve.

I study these image of life and beauty and begin to understand how people feel when seasons pass and nearly bury them with the remains of time.

On the bulletin board by my desk, I've posted my favorite picture of the November rose with its tattered petals and brilliant coral core.

Next to it is a newspaper photo of a very old woman I have never met. Her gray hair is covered and her skin is well-wrinkled.

Like the coral rose, her face tells far more than how many seasons have passed. The closed mouth and the eyes draw me deeper still to a spirit that has bent with the wind and held firm.

The flower and the woman are gone now. Their wisdom and beauty are not. The photos carry their message.

Escape from Technology

Last May, just before starting a 4-month sabbatical from this column, I shared my intention to escape from technology. I planned to make my body flexible again and treat my brain to history and politics rather than network configurations and security problems.

Indeed, during the first month, my computer remained idle except for email and internet searches. It was easy to allow these transgressions, as email is my main link to colleagues, and searching the Net is the fastest way to get information, period.

I searched for historical fiction books and ordered titles from the library or a bookstore. I hunted for biking trails and found I could request a free map of Seattle trails at www.seattle.gov/transportation/bikemapform.htm.

I ordered gifts online and read plenty of movie and book reviews.

My interest in politics led me to joining MoveOn.org and to read blogs such as WashingtonMonthly.com and DrudgeReport.com. I followed my favorite *New York Times* columnists at nytimes.com and international perspectives at news.google.com.

Away from the computer, I began taking loads of photographs. And, of course, that meant spending more time on the computer to edit and print the images.

A sabbatical is a great time to learn Adobe Photoshop, I decided, so I read *Adobe Photoshop CS: Classroom in a Book*, watched the Total Training video course and started dodging and burning images and doing the other tricks I haven't tried since I had a chemical darkroom two decades ago.

I also tried Microsoft's new Digital Image Studio 10 and the Epson Stylus Photo RX500 all-in-one printer. Time well spent, I figured, but I must get away from the computer, again.

While walking with my iPod mini one day, the battery ran out, again, so I decided it was time to try a MP3 player that lasts longer between charges. I tried several.

Besides trying new things, a sabbatical is a great time to do some massive cleaning and reorganizing. So, after totally cleaning and reorganizing the house, I decided to revitalize the computers. I followed the advice offered in articles and books about cleaning PCs and Macs. That helped, but I chose to reformat and reinstall my Mac operating system, and now it runs like new.

In the summer, my husband, daughter, and I go to our cabin every weekend, and during the long drive, my daughter likes to play games to pass the time. By chance, I discovered Schoolhouse Technologies Crossword Factory for creating crossword puzzles and used it to make some entertaining and challenging puzzles for her (and us).

The same child also went away to camp for two weeks. It was her first overnight camp experience, and to alleviate homesickness, I made silly photo postcards of family members so she could receive a picture and message from us almost every day. I used the postcard template at www.avery.com under the Software tab and printed on Avery's postcard paper No. 8387.

While she was away, my husband and I spent six days at our cabin without a phone or computer. We cut trails, hiked, read, and dreamed of doing it again. Indeed, we hoped our youngest would like camp well enough to go again next year.

That week away plus another that all three of us spent at the cabin were my only tech-free sabbatical. Almost every other day technology sneaked in. I invited it.

I've discovered technology isn't the bad guy. The bad guy happens to be me when I let technology suck all my time and energy. Over the past few months I've had the opportunity to get away from computers but never made a clean break because I didn't want to, and over time I've realized I don't need to if I can stay in control.

So, here I am, back again and ready to write about technology. My head is clear. I'm refreshed and ready to learn and to share some useful things. In the coming weeks, we'll cover computer cleanup, new music players, photo editing and much more. Stay tuned.

❈

Parenting Forever

This is another one of the "Getting Started" columns I wrote for *The Seattle Times* that involved explaining some aspect of personal technology to non-techie users, or getting new technology products from companies to use and review for the column.

Afterword:
Almost Two Decades Later...

The Family Affairs & Over Coffee columns in this book were written between 1997 and 2002 . . . starting almost twenty years ago. As our kids grew up, our parenting evolved from loving them, along with teaching our values, setting limits, and enforcing them, to guiding and supporting our kids in their efforts to lead their own lives, and eventually parent their own kids. Now, our parenting role is simply to love them, plus, support and advise when asked, listen when they want us to, lend money interest-free, watch movies together, host family gatherings, make coffee, iron karate gis, and more.

What's happened to us since I wrote those columns, besides adding more members to the family?

Parenting Forever

Justin graduated from college as a drama major. He also had a son, Landyn, while away at college, and took full responsibility for raising him. So, as a single father, Justin couldn't venture into the unsalaried world of acting, so he came home and tried several jobs before settling on a career that fits him well. He's a realtor, and rapidly becoming a rather successful one.

Several years after college, Justin met and later married Nicole, who was then a nanny, and now a fulltime mom for 13 year-old Landyn, and their 4 year-old son, Emmett. In her spare time, Nicole also volunteers for Friends of the Orphans, a local non-profit charity.

Justin's family enjoys spending weekends at our cabin in the mountains near Darrington, WA, when they're not at Landyn's baseball games or track meets, or spending time with Nicole's family.

Molly graduated from college as a psychology major, and later earned a Master's degree in early childhood education for children with special needs. Then she was hired as a teacher for young kids with disabilities in a local elementary school.

Besides work, Molly played rugby and enjoyed being part of its close community until she finally had to give it up after her second ACL injury.

Not so long after that, she met, and later married, Kathy, another sports enthusiast, who played softball in college, and currently works as a sales manager for a Seattle steel company. Molly and Kathy now have a 2 year-old daughter, Hadley, and a 2 month-old son, Keegan. So, with two very

Afterword: Two Decades Later

young ones, they don't get to many professional games anymore, but they do watch them on TV.

Abby is graduating from college this March with a double major in Japanese and Kinesiology, so she'll be receiving both Bachelor of Arts and Bachelor of Science degrees.

Because Abby never enjoyed playing the sports her siblings did—soccer or baseball—she explored new territory, and discovered karate in 4th grade. Since then, she has become a successful competitor in tournaments around the country and the world, and recently earned the honor of becoming a sensei.

Without a husband or kids, yet, Abby is free to roam the world and strive for further competence and recognition as a karate expert. Of course, she'll have to make enough money to support her adventures, but she'll manage.

Mike was a professor of Educational Leadership & Policy Studies at the University of Washington College of Education for over twenty-five years before retiring last year.

Hardly "retired," however, he continues to be extremely busy by supporting and promoting political, environmental, social, and multiple other causes, as well as attending classes at the Edmonds' Creative Retirement Institute. Plus, he's been teaching a class there on political cartoons.

Besides all that, he continues to design and build bridges to cross the creek behind our cabin in Darrington, WA, as well as write a book about building academic bridges, with examples from his own educational bridge-building across a long career.

Parenting Forever

Me? I wrote the columns in this book two decades ago, and now marvel at how much "things" have changed, in my life, in my kids' lives, and in the world.

After these parenting columns, I wrote a weekly column for *The Seattle Times* that focused on helping non-techie people learn how to use personal technology. In a few years, my column was syndicated by McClatchy publishing company, which was fun because friends and relatives around the country could occasionally read my column. The kids were happy to have me write it because I got a lot of free personal technology to try and then review, and if the companies didn't want their items returned, my kids often got them.

Then, in 2005, I suddenly got sick, fell into a coma for eight days, and woke up totally deaf, with my balance impaired, and my brain addled. It took almost a year to get better, acquire a Cochlear Implant so I could hear again, and for my brain to gradually rewire itself so it functioned normally again.

It was a tough time for Mike, who had to do everything for Abby at home, plus visit me daily, and try to get some work done. And it was tough for our kids—especially Abby, since she was just starting junior high school and didn't know whether her mom would ever wake up. Even when out of the coma, I was in rehab for three months before coming home. Then, we communicated by writing messages on white boards until I could hear again with help from a little computer implanted in my head.

A few months later, I started writing my *Seattle Times* column again, as well as two novels and a remembrance of the cycle of sickness to deaf & dumbness, to wellness again.

After previously publishing two books about educational technology with reputable publishers, and then

Afterword: Two Decades Later

not being able to find a publisher for my novels, I decided to publish them myself using CreateSpace. Great experience. Even better than publishing with an "official publisher" because I have more control over the book design and especially the book's cover design, while working with their excellent artists.

That's it for now. I'll be back with more parenting stories in another 20 years, maybe.

www.ingramcontent.com/pod-product-compliance
Lightning Source LLC
Chambersburg PA
CBHW061426040426
42450CB00007B/916